Recapturing the Biblical Epic of Prayer

Dr. Rob Finley

Recapturing the Biblical Epic of Prayer
Copyright ©1982, 2008 by Robert Finley
ISBN Paperback: 978-1-930285-45-3
Hardback: 978-1-941512-30-2
Ebook: 978-1-941512-31-9

Published by Master Design Publishing
789 St Rt 94 E, Fulton, KY 42041

**Additional copies of this book may be purchased from:
www.PrayerResources.org or www.MasterDesign.org**

Dr Finley's educational training includes degrees from Rhodes College, Southwestern Baptist Theological Seminary, and Luther Rice Seminary. His ministerial experience of pastoring Southern Baptist churches for twelve years and teaching Bible in Christian schools for seven years has provided a thorough command of Scripture capably communicated in both pulpit and writing forums. He has authored the encompassing manual on prayer entitled *Recapturing Biblical Intercession* and a six week preparation guide entitled *Meditations for Revival,* based on the 42 parables of Jesus. Dr. Finley has also written articles for several Christian periodicals.

To contact the author, please email rfinley@prayerresources.org

Scripture quoted from the King James Version are public domain.

Scripture quoted from the New American Standard Bible®, Copyright © 1960, 1962, 1963, 1968, 1971, 1972, 1973, 1975, 1977, 1995 by The Lockman Foundation. Used by permission." (www.Lockman.org)

All rights reserved. No part of this publication may be reproduced, stored in a retrieval system or transmitted in any way by any means, electronic, mechanical, photocopy, recording or otherwise, without the prior permission of the author, except as provided by USA and international copyright law.

Front cover image by David Teniers and used by permission of Kunathistorisches Museum, Wien, Austria.

Printed in the USA.

Acknowledgements

The acknowledgement page of a book is often skimmed over or totally ignored by the typical reader, but crafting an acknowledgement is a highly important task for the writer. Most, if not all, writers are limited to some degree or another in the overall publication of a book. Hence, acknowledging and communicating gratitude to those who have had a significant role in the publication is important. However, a word of acknowledgement is merely the tip of the iceberg of the gratitude that is being expressed. While I am grateful to the following for their role in preparing this book, my greatest joy comes in knowing that fruit has abounded to these co-laborers' account (Philippians 4:17)!

To my wife, Judy, my prayer partner and co-laborer of over 40 years: Absolutely without you by my side, this work would not have taken place.

To my daughter, Faithe: Your editorial oversight has immensely improved this publication of the message the Lord has established in my life. Thank you for your steady advice along the way!

To my two daughters, Faithe and Grayce, and their husbands, Kirk and Eric: Your prayers, valued counsel, and support have been a great source of encouragement. No greater joy comes to a father than to know that his children walk faithfully with the Lord!

To my grandchildren, Caitlyn, Eryn, Cameron, Ian, Lizbeth, and Mallie: The joy you have brought to my life has helped me to carry on amidst challenge after challenge. I pray that each of you will comprehend and apply the truths and principles set forth in this book.

To my dog, MacBeth: The always-growing mound of dog toys surrounding my computer chair has kept me mindful of your devotion and patience. Thank you for challenging me to be single-focused in pleasing the Lord (Colossians 3:22).

To the faithful board members and co-laborers of Prayer Resources: Your undergirding this ministry through love, prayers, and support has been indispensable for the accomplishment of this book and all the eternal fruit that it yields. Judy and I thank you from the bottom of our hearts.

THIS BOOK IS DEDICATED
To the Father's purposes
in preparing a Bride for His Son.

Table of Contents

1. The Purpose of the Universe: Prayer 1
2. Spiritual Warfare 4
   Satan, Secular Society, Sacred System, Sinful Self
3. Weapons Of Our Warfare 10
4. The History of Prayer 14
5. The Period of the Patriarchs 17
   Job, Abraham, Moses
6. The Period of the Judges 29
   Samson, Samuel
7. The Period of the Kings 35
   David, Solomon, Hezekiah
8. The Period of the Prophets 42
   Elijah, Isaiah, Jeremiah, Daniel, Habakkuk, Jonah
9. The Period of Christ 55
   The Pre-existent Christ, The Earthly Christ,
   The Ascended Christ
10. The Period of The Apostles 60
    The Apostles in Acts, Paul, James

Conclusion 66

Endnotes 67

Bibliography 70

Introduction

Introductions are important! Whether a person is being introduced to a new hobby, a new line of merchandise, or a new friend for the first time, gaining that introductory framework of knowledge is critical for any further development of participation, application, or relationship. A poor introduction can lead to misunderstanding and perhaps even rejection. If first impressions are false impressions, disharmony and defeat will follow. To miss the details of a proper introduction, however, leaves a person attempting to piece together the subsequent conversations, much like someone attempting to piece together a puzzle without the introductory picture.

What a privilege is mine to introduce to the reader the subject of prayer! To many readers, this will be like an introduction to someone that you have admired for years, but only from a distance. To most readers, the subject of prayer is one with which they are most familiar, but have never been properly introduced! As a result of the missed introduction, the practice of prayer is like putting together a thousand-piece puzzle without the picture. Many will spend their entire lifetime never knowing what genuine prayer really is.

Some readers who missed a proper introduction to Biblical prayer approach praying like someone who tastes a delicious dessert for the first time. Instead of savoring the taste, they seek to analyze the dessert's ingredients and miss the true taste. The hyper-Calvinist who takes the wonderful experience of prayer and doctrinalizes it until it becomes lifeless is like this dessert taster! Jesus indicated that His Father does not hear those who in vain think that they shall be heard for their much speaking (Matthew 6:7).

Other readers who missed a proper introduction to Biblical prayer have experienced prayer like someone who, meeting a drop-dead beauty, will spend his entire conversation in a shallow, flirty sort of way. The Charismatic who prays with flighty and often theologically shallow words are like this romancer. Jesus taught that His Father does not hear those who pray to be seen and heard by men who will be impressed by their emotional verbiage (Matthew 6:5).

Some readers who missed a proper introduction to Biblical prayer have been taught to *praywalk* and to go on prayer journeys. Often added to this teaching is the anti-Semitic *kingdom-praying*. Jesus corrected the praying-in-the-street type of praying of His day (Matthew 6:5). He rejected becoming king until He is recognized as such by the covenant people of Israel (John 6:15). He is not the King of the Church and there are no kingdom-churches. He is the Head of the Church and will be, when His kingdom comes, King of the Jews (Matthew 6:10)!

Sadly, those without a proper introduction to prayer approach praying from the standpoint of stale familiarity. They converse in prayer through oft-repeated sentences, like someone who retells an overly familiar story for the hundredth time. They are like the average church member who has learned by rote memory the clichés and prayer phrases and finds himself repeating the same words, intonation, and subjects without giving it a second thought. They pray in public without ever approaching the Father in private (Matthew 6:6-7).

In the Sermon on the Mount, Jesus sought to correct the improper prayer patterns of His day. Then in a stunning moment through what we commonly call The Lord's Prayer, He introduced the Father for the first time to those who had been praying all their lives (Matthew 6:9-13)!

Today there is much that is wrong Biblically about how people pray. The great problem lies in the fact that most have never been properly introduced to Biblical praying! As a result, unbiblical and anti-Jesus (anti-Christ) types of praying have robbed many of genuine communication with the Father.

We need to stop and properly introduce the reader to Biblical praying. In this book, *Recapturing the Biblical Epic of Prayer*, the reader is introduced to the great truths of prayer as unfolded in the early chapters of the Bible through the lives of the patriarchs, the judges, the kings, and the prophets of God. A brief introduction to Jesus' practice and teachings of prayer, as well as prayer during the times of the Apostles will be explored. From this proper introduction, the reader will begin to understand prayer and will reshape his prayer life to that of Biblical praying. From the great epic stories of Scripture, God introduces the reader to the vital subject of prayer. With that being said, may I introduce you to the Biblical epic of prayer!

Chapter 1
The Purpose of the Universe: Prayer

Centuries ago from a Roman prison the Apostle Paul wrote in Ephesians 3:9-12 that understanding history requires the understanding of the mystery which has been hidden from the beginning of the world but has now been revealed. This mystery reveals that God's eternal purpose of the universe from all eternity is the production and the preparation of a Bride for His Son Jesus. This Bride is joint-heir of all things with Christ and co-reigns throughout the universe. The Bride is the Church! Through becoming the Bride of Christ, the Church has gained access to the very presence of God the Father. From this position, the Church is the controlling factor in human affairs and the possessor of the balance of power not only in the social order, but also in the salvation of individual souls.[1]

This mystery is only understood with a backward glance over history to see God's eternal working principles as they are applied in the production, selection, and preparation of this Eternal Companion, the Church.[2] The Church, it would seem, is the center and motive of all God's activities from all eternity.[3] This look at history will reveal a primal rebellion in the universe, a contention over man, and an ultimate selection of the Bride.

To begin at the beginning is to begin before there was a beginning. The eternal God in His essence had a Son for Whom He desired to have a bride. God had to be most careful in the selection of this bride so that His choice would be a worthy companion for His Son. Therefore, God designed a test to determine His selection and then a training program to prepare this Bride to co-reign with His Son.

God acted boldly! He allowed a primal rebellion to break

out in the universe. There was war in heaven.[4] The rebellion spread like wildfire. Satan, the leader of the rebellion, withdrew one-third of God's created angels from heaven and chose the planet Earth to inhabit.[5] The choice of Earth was no random selection, because in the meantime, God had made the masterpiece of His creating strength by creating Man and placing him on Earth. Satan desired to involve Man in his rebellion. The first three chapters of Genesis describe Satan's strategy. The rebellion reached the point of spiritual warfare. Paul declares in Romans that mankind has rebelled against God with Man becoming the enemy of God.[6]

By accepting vain promises, man was deceived by Satan. There was very little to be gained from Satan through man's rebellion. God continued to forgive, love and accept man. He understood man's dilemma. Man now faced two options: to continue in the rebellion under the deceptive rule of Satan or to accept God's forgiveness, love, and rulership. Mankind became split over the dilemma. Part of mankind continued in the rebellion. The other part believed that God would accept them back. These "believers" chose to be on God's side. God's test for the selection of a bride was successful. Because man had a choice, God was able to determine His selection of a Bride by those who returned His love. Those who did accept God's love and God's Son would become the Bride. The selection still continues. The contention over man still wages. Peter, in I Peter 5:8, indicates that Satan has taken up warfare against all those who believe in God's forgiveness and love. Satan ruthlessly opposes the Bride as well as God's Son.

By giving man a choice, the selection of the Bride was complete from God's perspective. This selection initiated the preparation of the Bride for ruling and reigning with God's Son. God through His wisdom has designed the entire universe to cooperate together for the purpose of the Church's preparation to be the Bride.[7]

The Church on the basis of this selection has been given the power to overcome the enemy.[8] The preparation of the

Bride involves her being trained to overcome Satan. Because the crown is for the overcomer, the Church must learn the art of victorious, spiritual warfare.[9] This overcoming of evil forces is the Church's preparation for her assumption to the throne. In order for the Church to learn the "technique of overcoming", God ordained the program of prayer.[10] Hence, God's prayer program is His method of preparing the Bride for her future queenly role.[11] The responsibility and authority for the enforcement and administration of God's decisions on earth have been given to the Church.[12] Thus a fundamental and important principle in understanding the scheme of prayer in God's economy is that God has bound Himself unequivocally to answer the Church's prayers.[13]

The Church must pray! This is God's designed way for her to learn to rule. By God's own choice, all of the authority of His Son is wholly inoperative apart from the prayers of a believing and praying Church.[14] God's government in the affairs of the world and the role of the Church is tied up with intercession.[15] Thus, God has selected the Bride for the present as well as future enforcement of His Will.[16]

This is the mystery, hidden from the beginning of the world, but revealed by an imprisoned Apostle in a short letter to the Church of Ephesus.

Chapter 2
Spiritual Warfare

In the book **Satan Is No Myth**, Oswald Sanders has written, "The consistent theme of the Bible from beginning to end is the conflict between good and evil, between God and the devil. It begins in Genesis and ends with the devil in the lake of fire in Revelation 20. The intervening chapters depict the swaying tides of battle in conflict waged in the heavenly sphere as well as on earth."[1] Prayer is only properly understood as it relates to spiritual warfare. A great deal of the Old Testament is devoted to the wars of Israel in order to teach New Testament saints how to fight the good fight of faith.[2] Much Biblical truth will remain an unsolved riddle if the believer fails to grasp the significance of the great fact of prayer warfare against the powers of darkness.[3] S. D. Gordon stated, "In its simplest meaning prayer has to do with spirit conflict."[4] Prayer is a clash of rival authorities.[5] Prayer from God's side is communication between Himself and His allies in the enemy's country.[6] R. Arthur Mathews has written, "To my way of thinking, it takes conflict and the fact of an enemy to put prayer in perspective as a significant factor in furthering the cause of Christ."[7] In this contention, the intercessor should understand the enemies and their effects upon prayer. There are four enemies that contend with the intercessor in the area of prayer. These four are Satan, secular society, sacred systems, and man's sinful self.

Satan

The infernal enemy of prayer is Satan's sovereignty.[8] Because Satan knows that his time is short, he is concentrating all he has in a desperate, last-ditch attempt to defeat the purposes of God.[9] Erwin E. Prange ably wrote on this issue when he stated, "The strong man knows the timetable. He knows that his time is strictly limited. Before Christ comes again Satan will concentrate his attack upon those witnesses who are the greatest threat to his kingdom."[10] Satan stands in opposition to prayer as seen in Daniel 10:12-13 when he literally hinders the answer to Daniel's prayer. In the Scriptures, Satan is revealed as a deceiver (Revelation 12:9), a destroyer (Revelation 9:11), a dictator (John 14:30), and a debator (Revelation 12:10). In these roles, Satan opposes the praying of an intercessor.

The Deceiver

In prayer Satan is the great deceiver by causing believers to remain ignorant of prayer principles, prayer promises, and prayer petitions. As long as the intercessor remains ignorant of these areas of prayer, Satan has very little to fear from the intercessor's prayer life and the advance of Christ. Satan has effectively deceived the average Christian by keeping him from learning the operating principles of prayer. Likewise, most Christians do not even understand how prayer works. They remain uninformed as to the numerous Biblical promises concerning prayer which await fulfillment only by way of prayer. Satan has crippled the average believer by keeping him uninformed concerning prayer requests which are vital for God's program to be carried out. The intercessor cannot afford to remain in ignorance. He should learn the principles, promises, and petitions of prayer.

The Destroyer

In prayer Satan is the great destroyer by causing believers to be impatient with God's timing in answering prayer. The average Christian's faith is often destroyed because of his immaturity and impatience in God's timing in answering prayer. Soon he stops praying altogether. For the intercessor, God's timing in answering prayer is a time of overcoming the enemy and is God's tool to develop maturity in the intercessor. One must be reminded that there is no such thing as instant maturity.[11] The enemy is attempting with all his might to alienate the believer from God, to destroy his faith in Jesus

Christ, and to make him rebellious toward God.[12]

The Dictator

In prayer Satan is the great dictator or ruler by causing believers to have an independent spirit. The intercessor cannot maintain independence from God and be effective in prayer. An independent spirit and prayer are opposites. In order for the intercessor to pray effectively he must become dependent upon God. The average Christian is so independent from God that he has stopped praying or at least prays very little. This is Satan's plan. His sovereignty is exerted through the independent spirit of the believer. Dependence upon God is a must for the intercessor's spiritual vitality.

The Debater

In prayer Satan is the great debater by accusing believers of their forgiven sins and questioning their standing with God. Satan's accusations concerning past failures have caused the average Christian to become frustrated with his prayer life. The end result is that he soon loses a perspective of his standing with God. He begins to concentrate upon his condition rather than his position. The intercessor cannot function in this state. He must realize his position in Christ. Warfare is God's designed means by which He develops man. It forces the intercessor to rely upon his position in Christ.[13]

Secular Society

The external enemy of prayer is the secular society. Our society stands opposed to prayer by subtly opposing three necessary elements of prayer: silence, secrecy, and mystery.[14] These three elements have for almost a century been for the Church the stone which has been rejected in the building of media-edifices.[15]

Silence

Secular society is opposed to silence: a necessary element in effective dialogue. Indeed, silence is necessary to all effective dialogues no matter the discipline. Our technological society stands opposed to silence. Communication has become the "savior" of all sorts of dilemmas in marriage, therapy, international treaties, and business. The advertising industry and the medias especially oppose silence. The intercessor should learn to be silent and listen for the "still small voice" of God.

Secrecy

Secular society is aimed at exposure: a removal of secrets from our lives. Hidden-ness is necessary in the habitat of religion. The scientific mind desires to know all secrets. Gossip columns and magazines try to discover all about celebrities. The average believer, it seems, only prays in public. He prays very little if at all in secret. Prayers that are a pretense require an audience.[16] For the intercessor, his life hidden in Christ is the most important aspect to his spiritual growth and discernment. The Psalmist stated in Psalms 51:6 that it was in the hidden part or secret that the intercessor would discern wisdom.

Mystery

Secular society is opposed to the mysterious: a vitally important element in prayer. There has always been a bit of mystery in religion. The Bible speaks of several mysteries: Christ's incarnation (I Timothy 3:16), God's Kingdom (Luke 8:10), God's indwelling (I Timothy 3:9), Israel's blindness (Romans 11:25), Christ's return (I Corinthians 15:51), and the Gentile Church (Ephesians 3:4-9). Mystery, though, to the scientific mind is an irritating situation. Man does not want to admit that there exists anything beyond his comprehension. Man feels that he will in time discover all mysteries. This prerogative belongs to God alone (Luke 12:2). Modern man has lost a sense of the transient dimensions of reality. Prayer to the intercessor should always remain a mystery. It is always near, but always out of reach.

Sacred System

The fraternal enemy of prayer is the sacred system. What is called "organized religion" is fundamentally at odds with the supposedly spontaneous spiritually of our time. Whatever forces planned the strategy, they were indeed diabolically clever, for they recruited the leaders of the Church itself to actually carry out the attack.[17] The intercessor must be braced for the unexpected opposition from the religious systems through which he desires to minister. The sacred systems of organized religion have always been the enemy of true spirituality as seen in the lives of Jesus (Matthew 26:3-4), Jeremiah (Jeremiah 37:3; 26:8), Elijah (I Kings 13:1-32), John Huss, Martin Luther, William Tyndale, and many others. Like true spirituality, the intercessor who prays cuts across the grain of liturgical patterns and shakes the very tradition of the Church. Often established churches have placed prayer as a low priority. Jesus, however, equated the Church with a place of prayer (Matthew 21:13). Paul Billheimer reminds us of this priority in his statement that "any Church without a well organized and systematic prayer program is simply operating a religious treadmill."[18]

Sinful Self

The internal enemy of prayer is man's sinful self. Perhaps the greatest enemy is man himself. Often the believer gives too much credit to Satan for the failures in his own self. The average Christian suffers in his prayer life in at least six areas. First, he often fails in prayer because he *lacks confidence* and assurance that he is indeed forgiven of his sins and thus has access to God (Romans 8:15). Secondly, he may *lack courage* to boldly ask for the things of which his heart desires (Hebrews 4:16). He further fails in prayer because he may *lack concentration* while praying. He is unable to sustain attention upon a single object of his prayer (Psalm 57:7). Fourthly, the average Christian fails to continue praying because he *lacks personal conditioning.* Physically he is unprepared to continue praying for very long (Romans 12:1-2). Still another cause of failure in the personal prayer of the believer is a *lack of confession.* Most believers fail to gain and maintain a clear conscience (I John 1:9). Lastly, the *lack of self- crucifixion* or dying to self causes defeat in the prayer of the average Christian (Galatians 2:20). This dying is an advancement in the Christian life which the average believer refuses to grasp. The intercessor should pray with assurance and boldness. He should be physically fit to continue praying with sustained attention upon his request. The intercessor should maintain a clear conscience and be willing to die in order for his prayers to be heard and answered.

Prayer is the battlefield where all the battles are fought and won.[19] Here the intercessor claims the victory of the cross against his enemies. Each time he prays, he again applies Calvary's victory over the enemy. Whatever the intercessor gains in prayer is the enemy's loss. So that what he gains is in inverse proportion to the enemy's loss. One gains, the other loses; one loses, and the other gains.[20] This is true for each of the four enemies the intercessor faces in prayer.

Chapter 3
Weapons Of Our Warfare

Since Satan knows that his time is limited (Revelation 12:12), the believer must realize that the conflict will only intensify over the next several years. The history of civilization has reached the point when the most serious conflict of all must begin. In face of the appalling happenings of the present day, the believer is steadily compelled to realize that only through a fresh baptism of suffering can the Church be purged and fitted for the task which still confronts her in the evangelization of the non-Christian world. The decisive battle of Christian truth is yet to be fought.[1] Who, though, can be effective in this battle? The soldier who does battle with the forces of evil must be a spiritual man, for only he can understand the battle and the equipment necessary for it.[2] Thus, in this contention, the intercessor must understand the armor of his warfare. R. Arthur Mathews wrote to this point, "If we accept the fact that our role in life is that of soldiers, then we must drop our toys and become more acquainted with the weapons of our warfare."[3]

Battles are won only by the soldier who fights, and fighting involves the use of weapons. Unused weapons do not inflict causalities on the enemy nor win wars. Therefore, the ability and the will to use weapons is what warfare is all about.[4] In Paul's great "Prayer Epistle", the Book of Ephesians, he describes the Christian's armor in his concluding remarks on living the Christian life. Each piece of armor he lists is necessary equipment for the effective intercessor. In Ephesians 6:14-18, Paul lists the pieces of the soldier's armor: a belt of truth, a breast-plate of righteousness, shoes of the Gospel of peace, a shield of faith, a helmet of salvation, and the sword of the Spirit. The writings of S.D. Gordon enlighten the intercessor as to the role of each piece of armor. He wrote that there are six qualifications under the figure of the six pieces of armor. A clear understanding of truth, a clean obedient life, earnest service, a strong simple trust in God, a clear assurance of salvation, and a good grip of the truth for others. These things prepare a man for the real conflict of prayer. Such a praying man drives back the hosts of the traitor prince.[5] These pieces of armor in the intercessor's life merely equip him for the battle. The battle remains to be fought. Prayer is where the conflict is won or lost. This is the reason why Paul concludes this analogy by talking about prayer. This type of prayer involves spirit-fighting.

Notice again each piece of armor in light of spirit-fighting. The intercessor's continuous victory depends upon his knowledge and use of both defensive and offensive warfare. Defensive warfare is based upon several attitudes of the spirit. The intercessor should maintain a *teachable spirit* in order to gain a clear understanding of the truth. He should have an *obedient spirit* through a clean, pure life. The intercessor should develop a *servant spirit* by ministering in the simplest of opportunities. He should also have a *believing spirit* as exemplified in a strong, simple trust in God. The intercessor should through his *new spirit* gain a clear assurance of his salvation. The spiritual soldier thus equipped is now ready for the offensive conflict. This offensive conflict is two-fold. The intercessor through a *witnessing spirit* should have a good grasp of truth for others. The Word of God as ministered by the Spirit of God is to be used offensively. Also, the spirit in conflict is revealed as the intercessor in prayer. This is spirit-fighting.

Let's look at the pieces of armor again.
- The soldier should have a **belt of truth**: a clear understanding of the Truth and a *teachable spirit*. This weapon frees him to pray and keeps him from deception.
- The soldier should have a **breast-plate of righteousness**: a clean, obedient life and an *obedient spirit*. This weapon removes all hindrances to prayer and opposes

the sin in his life.
- The soldier should have the **shoes of the Gospel of peace**: a life of earnest service and a *servant spirit*. This weapon involves the believer in God's work, but he should look out for over-involvement.
- The soldier should have the **shield of faith**: a strong simple faith in God that produces the foundation of a *believing spirit*. This weapon of faith combats any doubts.
- The soldier should have the **helmet of salvation**: a clear assurance of his salvation that provides the believer with a new spirit that enables him to pray. This weapon dispels any doubts of salvation.
- The soldier should have the **sword of the Spirit**: a good grasp of the truth manifested through a *witnessing spirit*. This weapon gives him power in his prayers and combats any misunderstandings of the Word.
- The soldier should have a **life of prayer**: a *new spirit* of understanding that prayer is our greatest weapon and where the battle actually takes place. This weapon makes the Word effective. There is great opposition to this final aspect.

The chart on the following page may aid in understanding this subject.

Often the average believer fights physically, mentally, emotionally, and volitionally. Seldom does he fight with his spirit. "In its warfare against sin and Satan," wrote Robert Caldwell, "no weapon at the command of a living and purified Church is more effective than that of All Prayer, and yet how loathe we are to use it!"[6] Prayer is the one action of spiritual warfare. Prayer creates conflict. Prayer is the key to victory in the spiritual conflict of which the intercessor is involved. "Our part in the conflict," wrote R. Arthur Mathews, "is carried out in the effort of prayer."[7]

Weapons of Our Warfare in Ephesians

Pieces of Armor	Verse	Qualities Needed	Spirit	Meaning	Opposition
Belt	6:14	Clear Understanding of the Truth	Teachable	Frees Us to Pray	Deception
Breastplate	6:14	Clean Obedient Life	Obedient	Removes All Hindrances	Sin in the Believer
Sandals	6:15	Earnest Service	Serving	Involves the Believer	Over-Involvement
Sheild	6:16	Simple Trust in God	Believing	Becomes the Basis of Prayer	Distrust
Helmet	6:17	Clear Assurance of Salvation	New	Is Fundamental to Prayer	Doubts of Salvation
Sword	6:17	Grasp of Truth for Others	Witnessing	Gives Power in Prayer	Misunderstanding the Word
Prayer	6:18	Our Greatest Weapon	Spirit-Fighting	Makes Word Effective	Various Hindrances to Prayer

Chapter 4
The History of Prayer

As previously mentioned, prayer is not understood apart from its relationship to the Biblical purpose of the universe. Prayer is God's intelligently designed program for on-the-job training for ruling with His Son – both now and in the future – as His Bride and co-heir to the Father's throne. Overcoming involves spiritual warfare. Also previously mentioned was the fact that prayer is only properly understood as it relates to spiritual warfare. As the intercessor prays, he will create a conflict with several enemies. A third prerequisite to a proper understanding of prayer is to view prayer's relationship to Biblical history. Since prayer is God's predetermined plan to mature the Bride, one should expect to see that revealed in the Scriptures.

In understanding prayer and its relationship to Biblical history, three foundational principles should be mentioned. Since prayer is the primary means of apprenticeship for co-reigning with Christ:

1. then it would be logical to find prayer *spoken of in large measure* in the epic of both the Old Testament and the New Testament. An open and honest look at the Word of God will prove to be rewarding in this regard.
2. then it would also be logical to find prayer as the *central part of the lives* of those whom God used to shape both sacred and secular history. This too becomes obvious to the honest reader of Biblical truth.
3. then it would be logical to find prayer as the *basis for outlining Biblical history*. An overview of Biblical history will demonstrate the truth of this last statement. Prayer, as it relates to an overview

of Biblical history, is seen in an expansion of six historical divisions accompanied with personal examples in each division.

The Period of the Patriarchs is concerned with how one can *become an intercessor*. The Scriptures begin with a patriarch named Job, who is described as a man of prayer and intercession. The Bible continues the saga of the Patriarchs with Abraham and Moses, both of whom are continually portrayed as men of prayer. As one looks at the prayers of these three, he will notice a foundation of how one can become an intercessor.

The Period of the Judges takes an advance beyond the last period and is concerned with how the intercessor *overcomes the enemy* by the Spirit's empowering. Samson is seen as an ordinary man apart from his prayers and the Spirit's anointing. Samuel is beautifully pictured as a great man of prayer and intercession in overcoming the enemy by the Spirit.

The Period of the Kings is concerned with how to *co-reign with authority* in Christ through intercession. Two kings of the United Kingdom, David and Solomon, clearly demonstrate the principle of ruling through prayer. Hezekiah, a king of the Divided Kingdom, reveals how to co-reign with prayer and intercession.

The Period of the Prophets, including the Oral, Major, and Minor Prophets, is concerned with how intercessors *pray with discernment* into people and events. The Oral Prophet Elijah demonstrates very keenly his insights into the events and people of his day and also the priority of prayer in his ministry. The Major Prophets Isaiah, Jeremiah, and Daniel, reveal this same discernment for their times. The Minor Prophets Jonah and Habakkuk clearly show the discernment into events and people of their day.

The Period of Christ demonstrates how to *pray more effectively* by following Christ's example and teaching. A closer look at the Pre-existent, Earthly, and Ascended Christ will show the priority of prayer in the life and ministry of

Jesus both through example and teaching.

The Period of the Apostles is concerned with how to pray as intercessors *with a New Testament understanding and position.* The Apostles in general, along with Paul and James specifically, reveal the priority of prayer from the perspective of the risen Christ and His Spirit indwelling the believer and positioning the believer "in Christ".

The progression in the Biblical epic as revealed in the various Periods is God's program of maturing the believer for throne-ship with His Son. *Each intercessor should progress along these same lines.*

Chapter 5
The Period of the Patriarchs

The history of Biblical praying begins especially with the Period of the Patriarchs. In the Book of Genesis, we find that God spoke freely with Adam (Genesis 2:16-18; 3:8-13) and with Cain (Geneses 4:8-15). With the introduction of Seth, the Scriptures declare, "Then man began to call upon the name of the Lord" (Genesis 4:26 NAS). The Bible then speaks of Noah and God in a dialogue together (Genesis 6:13-21; 7:1-4; 8:15-17; 9:1-17). During this period of Biblical history man is being taught why and how to become an intercessor. This study will focus on the lives of Job, Abraham, and Moses.

Job

Intermittent with the Book of Genesis is the Book of Job. The central character of the book is the man named Job. He is a contemporary of the Patriarchs of the Book of Genesis. The book itself is foundational because of its triad of themes.

Understand The Insurrection In Heaven

The *insurrection in Heaven* is one of the themes of the Book of Job. This is given as the background to the life of Job as the intercessor. Job becomes a battleground between God and Satan, between heaven and hell, between the truth about human nature at its deepest and the lie the Devil is telling.[1] The book begins with a conflict between God and Satan over the man Job because of his uniqueness. Chapter one, verse five indicates that Job is unique because of his ministry of intercession. Prayer creates conflict and Job's prayers were certainly creating a conflict. Because God was answering his prayers, there was a hedge of answered prayers built around Job, hindering Satan's attack. Satan challenged God to remove the hedge of answered prayer. When God did this, Job experienced defeat, despair, and death of loved ones. Suffering followed in every area of his life: his family was broken apart, his friends misunderstood him, his financial assets were wiped out, and his body racked by disease. These calamities are often the results of lack of prayer but Job was experiencing them first-handedly though he was still praying (Job 16:17). It was God Who had chosen not to answer his prayers. The intercessor must be at peace knowing confidently that confronting opposition is part of his calling.

Have A Disciplined Life Of Intercession

Intercession in the life of Job is an additional theme of the book. This view is supported by Ezekiel's testimony concerning Job (Ezekiel 14:20). Job is revealed as God's key intercessor of his day. Throughout the book, Job's prayer life seems to be the crucial point of contention (Job 1:5; 5:1; 15:4; 16:19-21; 19:7; 21:15; 22:27; 27:8-10; 31:35; 42:8,10). Job described his life as that of an intercessor in Job 29. Day in and day out habits of prayer keep the intercessor in spiritual readiness for when opposition increases.

Recognize The Utter Hopelessness Without A Redeemer

The last theme of Job is that of *inquiry for a Mediator* (Job 9:32-33; 16:19-21; 31:35). Job, while suffering innocently, cried out for a Kinsman Redeemer or Mediator to plead his case before God. An essential principle of prayer becomes evident at this point: God will not do apart from prayer what He can do through prayer.[2] God's eternal desire was to send Jesus to redeem mankind and become man's Mediator (Revelation 13:8; 1 Timothy 2:5). God is seen in the Book of Job as programming the events of Job's life that would cause him to cry out in prayer for the very thing that God desired to do for him. Once the test of Job was removed, God set in motion His plan of the ages in answer to Job's prayers. Here in the Book of Job, it is shown that through an eternal conflict between God and Satan, man learned to overcome Satan through intercession and then to inquire before a righteous

God to send a Mediator or an Intercessor to plead his cause. Thus the Book of Job is foundational to one's understanding of prayer and the role of an intercessor.

Abraham

Genesis is the book of beginnings or firsts. In Genesis, God spoke of various things for the first time and He set a precedent for those words throughout the Scriptures. This is true for the word "prayer" as seen in the life of Abram. The word "prayer" first appears in this book in relation to Abram. Whatever a man professes to be will be tested by God to determine the genuineness and quality of that profession. Abram's life was tested over and over again. Since Abram was to be the Father of the Hebrew nation and since he was to demonstrate intercession, his profession had to be tested. The life of Abram can be divided into four areas depending upon what he was called at different times. This outline will yield deep insights into exactly how to become an intercessor.

Abram The Man

**Develop A Deeper Devotion
Toward God Than Toward Man**

While Abram is viewed as an ordinary man he reveals basic principles for becoming an intercessor (Genesis 12:1-14:12). Like Abram, the intercessor should have a deep devotion toward God. Abram was born into a heathen, polytheistic culture and yet he maintained a deep monotheistic devotion toward God. God called out to Abram and requested him to leave his country, home, and family members (Genesis 12:1-4). Abram heard God's calling, but failed by not separating himself from two spiritually demoralizing family members, Terah and Lot. If one is to become an intercessor he must overcome the influence of family members upon his devotional life. Often family relations can hinder the effectiveness of prayer in the life of God's people. Overcoming this hindrance is vital to an intercessor. The disobedience of Abram cost him five years of ministry in Haran. Although Terah died, trouble continually dogged his steps until Lot was finally removed. Then, God blessed Abram (Genesis 13:14). If an intercessor is to grow spiritually, he must place prayer as a priority in his life, even above the influence of family.

Trust God Rather Than Man For Provisions

It should be noted that in Genesis 12:7-8 Abram sought in Canaan first a place of worship before a place to live. With this priority established, he called upon the name of God in prayer. Having confidence in God's provision even in the midst of difficult circumstances should characterize a man of faith. A famine was in the land (Genesis 12:10). Abram failed in allowing God an opportunity to provide the necessities of life. He continued traveling until he arrived in Egypt. God had told him to go to the Promised Land, but Abram had gone through the Promised Land to the prosperous land of Egypt. While he was in Egypt, there is no reference to Abram's prayer life. Years were wasted! An intercessor should learn to allow God to provide life's necessities during difficult times.

Be Willing To Stand Alone

Abram finally returned to prayer after experiencing God's deliverance from Egypt. The intercessor should, like Abram, be willing to stand alone. Abram faced a test of not allowing worldly friendships to interfere with his devotion with the Lord. Abram and Lot were contrasting personalities. God delights in placing contrasts next to each other in the Scriptures: Samuel and Saul, Jesus and Judas, Jacob and Esau, David and Solomon, Hezekiah and Manasseh. These two personalities, Abram and Lot, could not dwell together. Lot is a type of the world. Abram is a type of godliness. These two had to separate or Abram would face spiritual defeat. Abram's decision to have a deep devotion toward God, to have confidence in God's provisions in the midst of difficult circumstances, and to be willing to stand alone, enabled him to become a great intercessor. To this man, God has promised a land and a nation

(Genesis 12:2-3).

Abram The Hebrew

In Genesis 14:13, the Bible speaks of *Abram the Hebrew*. This is the first time the word "Hebrew" appears and it is associated importantly with Abram, the Father of the Hebrews. In this section of Genesis, the Bible describes principles for a growing intercessor.

Overcome Past Failures

Like Abram, an intercessor should learn to overcome the consequences of past failures. Abram's past failure in bringing Lot with him out of Ur had later consequences. Abram had to learn to love the unloving. Lot was a constant reminder of his failure in obeying God. Lot had watched Abram fail in obedience and had built in his own life a habit of disobedience. The test of character is not in never failing, but in getting back up after one has failed. Abram had to overcome his personal feelings toward his nephew if he was to grow in prayer.

Guard Against Temporal Things Overshadowing Spiritual Things

The intercessor should also value spiritual things over temporal things. In Genesis 12:16 and 13:2, the Bible states that Abram was rich as a result of his Egyptian sojourn. One of the consequences of being out of fellowship with God in Egypt was his becoming wealthy. Materialism, however, often robs people of their spiritual life. The preoccupation with raising cattle and growing a family had taken their toll upon Abram's spiritual life. In Genesis 14:17-24, Abram was faced with temptation to become even richer by the King of Sodom. As a man of prayer, he had to become the possessor of his possessions instead of his possessions possessing him. Abram had to learn to place spiritual things over temporal things. The intercessor should likewise learn the priority of spiritual things. The intercessor should also reject worldly advice and methods. Abram followed the worldly advice of his wife in having a child through Sarah's Egyptian handmaid named Hagar. God's way was for Sarah, not Hagar, to have a child. Failure in following God's plan resulted in the birth of Ishmael. The intercessor should learn to overcome worldly advice and methods which so often subtly establish strongholds in our lives. To Abram the Hebrew, God renewed His promises of a child (Genesis 13:14-18; 15:1-18).

Abraham The Spiritual Leader

Overcome Periods Of Silence

When Abram was 99 years old, God changed his name to Abraham and designated him as a spiritual leader for the whole world (Genesis 17:5). Between chapter sixteen and chapter seventeen, there is a thirteen-year gap of silence. Abram was not praying and God was not speaking. Finally in God's own timing, the silence was broken. In order for Abraham to become a leader and a man of prayer, he had to overcome this time of silence. The thirteen years of silence were years of spiritual depression for Abram, but he experienced a spiritual crisis in his life that left him a changed man. Even his name reflected his experience. Following this experience, he was known as Abraham, instead of Abram.

Abram's period of silence is not unique in Scripture. Between Malachi and Matthew, there is a period of over four hundred years of silence when God sent no prophet to His people. As a result, a small remnant of Jews turned to the Old Testament for insights. It was this preparation that God used when He sent His Son Jesus. The period of silence proved to be profitable. The intercessor should overcome the times of drought in his own life if he is to mature and become a spiritual leader.

Mature In Love For Others

Abraham had already rescued Lot out of Sodom once. In fact, Abraham had to go to war in order to save Lot. This nephew had failed a second and third time. Abraham had to struggle with the question of whether or not to rescue Lot one more time. His maturing love would not allow him to turn his back on his wayward relative. Abraham became bold with God in interceding for Lot and Sodom (Genesis 18:22-33). A man of intercession will always be overcome by his patient and sacrificial love for others.

Abraham The Prophet

Pray For Your Enemies

When Abraham became an intercessor for his enemy Abimelech, he was no longer just a spiritual leader (Genesis 20:7). He was called a prophet of God. He was a praying man. It is at this point that the word *prayer* is first mentioned in the Bible. Abraham here illustrates progressive stages in the life of an intercessor. An intercessor should experience a death to self as did Abraham. To become an intercessor, one must die to himself. This is an advance beyond being separated from home and family. An intercessor must die to himself. Even though Abraham was a spiritual leader, he allowed an unresolved conflict to crop up once again in his life. Abraham failed as he had previously done. Abraham again journeyed to Egypt and placed his life in jeopardy because of his deception about his identity. God said that He would spare Abimelech's life if Abraham would pray for him. Not only is this occasion the first mention of the word "prayer", it is also the first time the word "prophet" appears in the Scriptures. God constantly points out in Scripture that one of the signs of a true prophet is prayer (Jeremiah 27:18). It was not by accident that they appear first together. Abraham's ministry at this point was that of a prophet and also an intercessor. Abraham's prayer was for someone else and not for himself. He had died to the selfish desires of the flesh. Abraham brought healing through prayer. Like Abraham, the intercessor should pray for even his enemies. Regardless of his personal feelings toward

Abimelech, Abraham prayed for the healing of the man. Abraham was positioned by God to pray for his enemy. This could only be done by love.

Continue To Mature In Faith

Though Abraham had matured from being just a man to being a prophet in his prayer life, he had needed to overcome many failures throughout his life. Instead of allowing his failures to diminish his faith, he used overcoming his failures to increase his faith. When he faced the greatest struggle of his life in Genesis 22, he had reached a level of maturity in his faith that yielded great victory. He was tempted or tried at the point of his commitment toward God with the apparent sacrifice of his son, Isaac. His faith that God could even raise Isaac from the dead was a bold step toward maturity. A faithful intercessor will, at one time or another, be tested by God concerning his commitment to prayer. That testing may be draped in horror as vivid as Abraham's testing; yet, as the intercessor has learned to mature from faith to faith, he can know great victory.

Moses

After Abraham, the next great Patriarch to illustrate how to become an intercessor is Moses. The Bible speaks of his greatness in prayer in two locations outside the Pentateuch. In Jeremiah 15:1 (NAS), the Scriptures teach, "Then the Lord said to me, 'Even though Moses and Samuel were to stand before Me, my heart would not be with this people; send them from My presence and let them go!'" Again in Psalm 99:6 (NAS), the Bible states, "Moses and Aaron were among his priests, and Samuel was among them that called on His name: they called upon the Lord, and He answered them." Moses' greatness in prayer is further emphasized in Deuteronomy 34:10. Here it states, "Since then no prophet has risen in Israel like Moses, whom the Lord knew face to face." (NAS). The phrase "face to face" is an expression implying prayer. Through his prayer life, this Patriarchal Prophet delivered Israel out of Egypt, split the Red Sea, received the Ten Commandments, organized the building of the Tabernacle, laid the foundation of the priesthood, separated the feast days and sacrifices for the Hebrews, and wrote the Pentateuch. There was no one to compare with Moses – except, of course, Jesus (Hebrews 3:1-6). In Deuteronomy 18:15 (NAS), Moses declared, "The Lord your God will raise up for you a prophet like me from among you, from your countrymen, you shall listen to him." Jesus was greater than Moses for one reason – His prayer life was greater. Jesus delivered man from eternal judgment, fulfilled the Ten Commandments, was the Tabernacle of God, became the great High Priest forever, sanctified the Passover, and became the Word of God in fulfillment. Jesus completely overshadows Moses! It is valuable, however, to gain from Moses insights into how to become an intercessor. The ministry of Abraham was to demonstrate the areas of prayer concern for the intercessor. A balanced prayer ministry must include the proper prayer concerns with the proper character qualities to support the prayers. A study of the life of Moses reveals several areas of responsibility for the intercessor.

Intercede For Victory In Spiritual Warfare

The intercessor should pray like Moses did in order to overcome the enemy in spiritual warfare. Insights into this principle are to be seen as one looks at the seventeenth chapter of Exodus. Israel had just come out of Egypt and had camped at Rephidim. The Israelites had run out of water. Moses provided water for God's people by striking a rock with the rod of God. This new source of water caused Amalek to attack Israel over water rights. This is the first time that Israel as a nation had engaged in war. As the Israelites, led by Joshua, fought in the valley against the Amalekites, Moses positioned himself on a nearby mountain and prayed for victory. Joining Moses in prayer was Aaron (the future High Priest) and Hur (the grandfather of Bezaleel, the first man mentioned that was filled with the Spirit of God; later Bezaleel became builder of the Tabernacle). Through Moses' prevailing in prayer, Israel won a great victory. So important was the victory that God told Moses to write down details of the victory for the sake of Joshua. This is the first of the writings of Moses. Moses also erected an altar, the first since the time of Jacob. The principle that the Lord desires the intercessor to learn from this chapter is that spiritual warfare is won through prayer.

Intercede For Deliverance From Sin

In Exodus 32, Moses is shown in the role of an intercessor as he pleaded with the Lord to be merciful toward Israel. This is a further principle for the intercessor to learn. The intercessor should pray for people whose lives are caught in sin and idolatry. In this chapter of Exodus, Joshua informed Moses of the sin in the camp. Apparently Joshua was half way up the mountain waiting prayerfully for Moses' descent. Moses made intercession with the Lord for Israel by reminding God of past deliverances, His present plan for the nation of Israel, His changeless love, His continual commitment to His covenants, and His eternal promises toward Israel. Through Moses' intercession God spared a large segment of the Israelite population.

Intercede For God's Presence

In the succeeding chapter, the great Tabernacle had been built, but it remained empty. Moses prayed and God filled the Tabernacle with His presence. The principle demonstrated in this chapter is that, like Moses, the intercessor should pray for God to fill His House with His presence. Intercessors should be concerned with God's presence in corporate worship.

Intercede For National And Personal Revival

This same chapter of Exodus reveals the principle that the intercessor should pray for the revival of his nation. Chapter thirty-three of Exodus describes the first national revival in the history of mankind. Moses' prayer in Exodus

32:32 is answered by the Lord in Exodus 33:1. The revival followed Moses' prayer and progressed over several steps of action: awareness of sin, repentance of sin, obedience to God, separation from evil, renewal of worship, restoration of God's chain of authority, establishment of prayer priority, and renewal of family worship. In Exodus 33:12-23, Moses prayed for his own personal revival.

Intercede For The Necessities Of Life

Another principle of intercession in the life of Moses is found in Numbers the eleventh chapter. Like Moses, the intercessor should pray for the necessities of life. Through the prayers of Moses, Israel was sustained in the wilderness for forty years. Over one million people were fed manna or quail and water daily over that period of time through the prayers of Moses.

Intercede For Physical Healing

In the twelfth chapter of Numbers, Moses is described as praying for the healing of Miriam. Here the intercessor learns to pray for physical healings of those who are sick. As shown in the life of Abraham in Genesis twenty, so it is revealed again in the life and ministry of Moses. Miriam had become leprous because of disobedience and sin. Moses, however, interceded for her and she was made well.

Intercede For Salvation

The last principle in the life and ministry of Moses for the intercessor is to be found once again in chapter 32 of Exodus. The intercessor should pray for the lost of mankind and for God's means for reaching them. Moses prayed for the forgiveness of the sins of those who had rebelled against God. Moses cried out in verse 32 (NAS), "But now, if Thou wilt forgive their sin – and if not, please blot me out from Thy book which Thou has written!" God answered Moses' prayer and delivered a remnant of faithful Israelites.

Thus it becomes evident in the life of Moses, that the

intercessor should pray for victory over the enemy, deliverance of those trapped in sin, God's presence in worship services, a great awakening of a nation, the necessities of life, physical healings, and the salvation of the lost.

Chapter 6
The Period of the Judges

The next great lessons on prayer are to be found in the Biblical Period of the Judges. A study of the Book of Judges reveals a five-step cycle that repeats itself seven times throughout the book (Judges 3:5-11; 3:12-30; 4:1-5:31; 6:1-8:32; 8:33-10:5; 10:6-12:15; 13:1-16:31). Each time Israel failed to obey Moses' instructions found in Deuteronomy chapter six and Joshua's reminder found in Joshua chapter twenty-three, they would repeat the cycle. This disobedience on the part of Israel included: intermarrying with the heathen, worshipping the heathen's idols, not driving the heathen out of the land, and not keeping the commandments of the Lord. Their disobedience would lead them into the five step cycle of: the sin of idolatry, the disciplined suffering by the hand of an enemy nation, the supplication of Israel for a deliverer, the salvation through a judge, and then the silence of peace. Seven times in the Book of Judges Israel fell into this cycle!

The Bible states that enemies were left in the land to test or prove the Israelites. They were a necessary corrective to produce maturity in Israel. The Book of Judges was written with the intention of instructing God's people on how an intercessor can overcome the enemy by the power of the Spirit. God's plan involved an opportunity for His people to pray. Once Israel experienced the pressure of suffering, the people prayed. God honored their prayers and sent a judge. Israel, having been delivered, then enjoyed peace and security to the point of turning to silence. They stopped praying! When they stopped praying, they fell into sin again. The cycle would begin all over again.

The nation was slow in learning the principle that prayer is God's priority and program. Prayer was the only proper and acceptable response to the suffering that God sent. God's approach to Israel was to create opportunities for prayer. This is His approach to other nations as well. Prayer provides the victory! The Book of Judges speaks of fourteen judges. In addition, there are five judges mentioned in the Book of 1 Samuel. These judges were sent in answer to prayer alone. These judges overcame the enemies of God by the Spirit's empowering through prayer. Prayer emphasis is seen in the lives of many of the judges. Much could be said of the prayer of Deborah (Judges 5) and of Gideon (Judges 6); but our focus in this division will be concentrated upon Samson and Samuel as they clearly demonstrate the intercessors overcoming through prayer.

Samson

The life of Samson illustrates how the intercessor overcomes the enemies by the Spirit's empowering especially toward the end of his life. Samson is a controversial figure in the Bible. Often he is seen as a Spirit filled judge. At other times he is seen as a carnal follower of the one true God. Avoiding the controversy and looking at Samson as an intercessor, a study of Samson's role as an intercessor reveals important concerns for the serious intercessor of today.

Commit To A Disciplined Way Of Life

The intercessor should, like Samson, make a commitment to a way of life that would be of God's choosing (Judges 13). Not all of God's intercessors were called to be Nazarites. The intercessor should, however, discover God's design for his own life and then, through obedience and overcoming failures, follow that plan God has for his life. God's design is for each intercessor to be an individual uniquely positioned in a strategic situation in order to bring about God's will in that given situation.

Depend Upon The Holy Spirit

A life of dependence upon the Spirit's anointing and empowering should characterize the intercessor. This principle in the life of Samson stands out perhaps more than any other. Samson did not rely upon fleshly, carnal weapons to fight spiritual conflicts. To Samson, all conflicts were spiritual ones. God's anointing upon Samson was the pathway to victory.

Gain Victory Over Failures

The intercessor should also overcome past failures and resolve problematic youth conflicts. Samson often overcame small numbers of the enemy, but it was in the end of his life that he would gain his greatest victory. He had prepared his life for overcoming great difficulties. He is an illustration for the intercessor of overcoming the smaller conflicts in order to be prepared for the greater ones.

Destroy Strongholds

Like Samson, the intercessor should overcome the strongholds in his life. This principle became an all important area for Samson. Through opening up his life to the flesh and through yielding to temptations of Satan, Samson had allowed some strongholds of carnality to build in his life. After much suffering Samson overcame these temptations. The intercessor, no doubt, has experienced this same difficulty. The strongholds should be routed out and destroyed. Then the intercessor should get into a position of spiritual influence. God will assist the intercessor at this point.

Die To Self

Samson finally achieved the strategic position of striking the winning blow against God's enemies. Although he died in the process, through prayer, Samson's victory was accomplished. His position of influence was greater than any position of authority that he might have gained. Like Samson, the intercessor should experience a death to self in order to serve the Lord more effectively. Samson died to self spiritually before he died physically. The decision was made. God honored both the decision and the prayer of Samson. God intends to honor the intercessor who will die to self in order to serve God through prayer. In Revelation 12:11, the overcomers of Satan are victorious because they loved not their lives unto the death!

Samuel

Samuel is a bridge character in the Bible. He is the key link in joining together the Judges, Kings, and Prophets. Although Samuel was not the last judge, he was the last of the great judges. The life of Samuel further illustrates how the intercessor overcomes the enemies of God by the Spirit's empowering.

Learn From Others Who Pray

The introduction of Samuel into the Biblical record is important. Samuel was born to praying parents (I Samuel 1). He undoubtably learned much from them concerning prayer. When possible, the intercessor should seek to learn from praying parents. Not all great intercessors will be so blessed as to have praying parents. Those that do are most fortunate indeed. Hannah, Samuel's mother, was so deep into prayer and intercession that the spiritual leader of her day did not discern or understand her approach to prayer (I Samuel 1:13). In fact, even her husband did not fully comprehend her burdened prayer (I Samuel 1:8). Because of her prayer, Samuel owed his existence first to supernatural factors, secondly to biological laws. The Lord had shut up Hannah's child-bearing potential. The power of prayer by Hannah moved God to lift His restraints.[1] When God desires to awaken a nation spiritually, He usually begins with a praying mother. The results of Hannah's prayers Samuel was: God's prophet to anoint Israel's first two kings; God's judge to rule over Israel and bring about peace from her enemies; God's prophet to train young prophets in the school of prophets in Bethel and Gilgal; and God's author of perhaps two important books in our Bible.[2] Indeed, the Hebrews view Samuel as a second Moses!

Develop Definite Prayer Habits

Another principle of prayer as seen in the life of Samuel is that the intercessor should seek to develop definite prayer habits in his early life (I Samuel 3). Samuel learned to communicate with the Lord as a small boy. This communication led to prayer habits that developed into a life style. Like Samuel, the intercessor should seek to be around spiritual people. Hannah was wise in investing the life of her son at the Temple under the experienced High Priest named Eli. Samuel learned much by being around this spiritual leader. Today's intercessor should seek out godly individuals to learn from them the ways of the Lord. The years of knowledge and experience of spiritual people should not be by-passed. The intercessor should further seek to mature his ministry by overcoming the enemies by the Spirit's empowering as Samuel did (I Samuel 7).

Position Yourself Between God and Man

Samuel's prayer life brought victory to Israel and defeat to the Philistines. In 1 Samuel chapter seven, the ministry of the intercessor is clearly outlined. Samuel instructed the people through exhortation on the subjects of conversion, cleansing, and commitment (verses 3-4). Samuel intervened for the people as seen in the communion, consecration, contrition, and confession of the people. Samuel enquired before the Lord in behalf of his people (verse 5). Samuel then interpreted through edification the contention of the people of God with their enemy and the chastisement of the people of God by their enemy (verse 6). Next, the inspiration of the example of Samuel through prayer caused the people of God to seek his counsel (verse 8). Samuel's intercession and entreaty before the Lord led to the conquest and the celebration of the people. Lastly, the illumination and enlightenment received by Samuel through prayer brought consolation to the people of God. This chapter is literally impregnated with spiritual truths concerning prayer.

Disciple Others In Prayer

Still another principle of intercession as seen in the life of Samuel is that the person of prayer should seek to expand his ministry through others. Samuel had a ministry of training young prophets through the school of prophets. The results of this training are seen in the explosive section of the Scriptures concerning the prophets. It is Samuel's influence that gives rise to the official position of a prophet. Intercessors today should seek teachable people and initiate prayer times with these people.

Embrace New Prayer Opportunities
Through Diminished Activities

Another principle of intercession in the life of Samuel is the intercessor recognizing each new opportunity as his greatest opportunity of service. Samuel resigned from the active ministry of leadership and chose the ministry of prayer (1 Samuel 8). What appeared on the surface to be the end of a great ministry became the beginning of a new opportunity in the life of Samuel to be used of the Lord in the area of prayer. Samuel's ministry of intercession caused the people to seek him out for prayer (1 Samuel 8). Through God's permissive will, Samuel guided Israel to a king. This produced many devastating results as the prophet had predicted. In fact, Samuel had prophesied that the day would come when even the prayer of the people of God would not be heard (1 Samuel 8:18). There is no mention of God hearing and answering the cries of Israel until they again sought out Samuel and requested him to pray for them (1 Samuel 12:19-23).

Samuel was a great man of prayer as attested to by the Psalmist in Psalm 99:6 (NAS), "Moses and Aaron were among His priests, and Samuel was among those who called on His name; They called upon the Lord, and He answered them."

Chapter 7
The Period of the Kings

From Samuel, the study on prayer naturally progresses to the study of the kings. There were forty-two kings of the nations of Israel and Judah during the times of the Kings. Included are three kings of the United Kingdom, nineteen kings of the Northern Kingdom of Israel, and twenty kings of the Southern Kingdom of Judah. This last group included one queen. Of the three kings of the United Kingdom, David and, to an extent, Solomon were outstanding kings in their prayer life. Of the Northern Kingdom of Israel, there were no great praying men. The kings were all evil. The Southern Kingdom of Judah, however, could boast of eight good kings: Asa, Jehosophat, Joash, Amaziah, Azariah, Jotham, Hezekiah, and Josiah. From these good kings, Hezekiah was the greatest in the area of prayer. This study on prayer will concentrate on David, Solomon, and Hezekiah.

David

The division of the Kings is concerned with how to co-reign with authority through intercession. This co-reigning is well illustrated in the life of David. In several different areas, David sets the example of an intercessor and illustrates praying with authority.

Begin Praying Early In Life

The intercessor should begin learning the priority of prayer early in his childhood. It is apparent that David spent much time meditating with the Lord as a young boy. David reflected the same maturity early in life that Samuel exemplified through learning to pray as a young boy.

Gain A Position Of Spiritual Authority

The intercessor should also seek to learn the position of

authority in prayer. David showed a great deal of discernment and wisdom in his steps toward ruling as king of Israel. In his rise to the throne, David sought every opportunity possible for advancement: victory over Israel's feared enemy Goliath, friendship with the king's son, marriage to the king's daughter, the sparing of the king's life, the capture of Jerusalem, additional political marriages with foreign monarchs, the moving of the ark to Jerusalem his capitol, and the restoration of King Saul's family to a respectable position in the kingdom. Spiritually speaking, David's rise to the throne was reflected in many of his Psalms (Psalms 2, 7, 9, 43, 52, 54, 56, 57, 59, 109, 140, 141, 142). Although the intercessor may not be called upon by God to advance to an office of authority, he will be called upon to advance to a spiritual position of authority.

Mature In Prayer Through Overcoming Discouragement And Failures

David's prayer life was also growing. The Psalms reflect a maturing attitude in praying with authority. The intercessor should begin to exercise the throne-rights of the intercessor in co-reigning with Christ. Just as David exercised his throne-rights, so should the believer. The Scriptures reveal that David sought the Lord's direction as the leader of Israel (2 Samuel 5:18-23; 7:18-29; 1 Chronicles 21:17-30). David had to learn to pray authoritatively. By overcoming discouragement and sin, the intercessor should also mature as a person of prayer. David experienced deep sin and failure in his life. David, however, overcame the discouragements and found victory through prayer (Psalm 51, 32, 3). The believer who desires to be used of God as an intercessor must learn to overcome discouragement and failure.

Give Prayer Priority In Old Age

Lastly, the intercessor should make prayer the priority of his ministry, and continue to do so even in the later years. David sought in his old age to make a House of Prayer unto the Lord. He commissioned two thousand Levites to praise and pray unto the Lord from morning until evening at the Tabernacle (1 Chronicles 23:30). David's final emphasis was on prayer (1 Chronicles 29:10-19). When all is said and done concerning the ministry of David, seventy-three Psalms are to be ascribed to him! David prayed as he ruled – as a king with authority.

Solomon

As in the case of David, Solomon also illustrates how to co-reign with authority through intercession. Solomon took up where David left off. He constructed a House of Prayer for God.

Seek God's Wisdom

Solomon's first step in building a strong prayer life as a king was to ask God for wisdom in co-reigning with authority (1 Kings 3:3-15). In order to be successful as an intercessor, one must have spiritual discernment and wisdom from God. Solomon asked God for this and it was given him.

Establish A Special Place For Prayer

Solomon's prayer life was made stronger by the selection of a special place of prayer. He built the Temple on Mount Zion (also called Mount Moriah), the location of Abraham's prayer altar for Isaac! Solomon called it a *House of Prayer*. He recognized the need for a quiet place to pray. In Solomon's prayer of dedication of the Temple he declared six distinct times that the Temple was specifically designed as a place of prayer (2 Chronicles 6:22, 24, 26, 28, 32, and 34). The intercessor should designate a special place to be his house of prayer.

Maintain A Primary Focus On The Needs Of Others

Solomon's dedication prayer in the Temple not only reflected having a special place for prayer, but it also exemplified his ministry of prayer for others. The intercessor should make prayer for others his main focus as did Solomon at this time in his life. It is sad to note that when Solomon began to taste of his great success as king, his eyes turned from others and began to focus on satisfying his own selfish lusts. The intercessor must always be alert to selfish leanings in his prayers and quickly refocus to others.

Hezekiah

The life of Hezekiah further illustrates how to co-reign with authority through intercession. Through the office and authority of the king, Hezekiah brought about reform and restoration to the Temple worship, feasts, offerings, and the priestly office. Hezekiah was a man of prayer (2 Chronicles 29:3; 30:18-27; 32:20-26). His prayer life is an example to the intercessor in a few specific areas.

Encourage Others To Pray

The intercessor should seek to influence others concerning the priority of prayer. Hezekiah desired to have as his first public, official act as king to be the opening again of the Temple, the House of Prayer (2 Chronicles 29:3). He desired for everyone in his kingdom to acquaint themselves with this House of Prayer. The intercessor should strive to influence others to have their priority the area of prayer. He should influence the Church to return to the Biblical priority and emphasis of prayer.

Pray With Others

Like Hezekiah, the intercessor should also seek to pray with those who are themselves great men of prayer (2 Chronicles 32:20). Hezekiah sought to pray with the prophet Isaiah, a tremendous man of prayer. Perhaps the greatest lessons the intercessor can learn in the area of prayer are those that are learned by praying with those who know how to pray. Hezekiah grew in prayer through Isaiah's influence to the point that he even surprised Isaiah with the power of his prayers. On one occasion Hezekiah was told by the prophet Isaiah that he was going to die. The king prayed unto the Lord and requested that he be given an extension on his life. God heard his prayer and extended his life by an additional fifteen years (2 Chronicles 32:24-26). Isaiah did not anticipate Hezekiah's prayer, nor God's response.

Value Life For The Purpose Of Prayer

The intercessor should overcome hindrances that could shorten his ministry. Hezekiah's ministry was threatened to end if he did not seek to overcome this threat of death. Hezekiah was not finished in his responsibilities to Israel. He cried out to God for an additional number of years to be added to his life, and his ministry was extended. Intercessors often stand in crisis situations because of their unique responsibility in prayer. Satan opposes the effective intercessor. Satan seeks every opportunity to shorten the ministry and life of God's intercessor. The intercessor should overcome this opposition in order to continue his ministry of prayer. Great is the value of the prayers of the elderly and the infirmed! It is Satan who seeks to end their lives and cut short their influence. Even the mentally infirmed seem to have a supernatural ability through their spirit to cry out to the Lord.

David, Solomon, and Hezekiah are but three of the kings that were men of prayer. Time and space limits a deeper study into their lives and the lives of the other kings. Five overriding principles appear to stand out concerning the kings.

An acute search for discernment surfaces as a principle that appeared in the lives of many of the kings. The lives of David (2 Samuel 2:1) and Solomon (1 Kings 3:3-14) illustrate this truth. The intercessor of today should seek to have discernment in his praying (Ephesians 2:5-6; Romans 8:34; James 1:5-6).

An absolute surrender to God for the work of prayer appears as a principle of prayer in the lives of several of the kings. This surrender involves foundational commitments of one's life: a union with God in prayer (John 15:7; Psalm 37:4; 1 Chronicles 29:12), a cooperation with His workings through prayer (Psalm 20; 2 Samuel 15:31; 1 Chronicles 29:10-19), an entrance into God's plan through a prayer ministry (Psalm 39:22; 2 Timothy 2:7), and a definite claim upon Biblical promises through prayer (Psalm 42:5, 11; Psalm 43:5).

The principle of *an authentic submissiveness to God* appears to be evident in the prayer lives of the praying kings. A genuine brokenness that resulted in sincere confession certainly characterized these kings (2 Samuel 12:16; 2 Samuel 24:10; Psalm 51; Psalm 32; 1 Chronicles 21:17).

Authoritative supplication in the House of God also characterized the praying kings. In fact, the Chronicler sought to evaluate the success and effectiveness of the kings according to how they related themselves to the Temple, the House of Prayer. Those kings who spent time in prayer in God's House, were evaluated with praise and adoration. Since prayer is on-the-job training for ruling with Christ, it comes as no surprise to find that the kings should be evaluated by their faithfulness to the one ministry that is above all ministries – prayer.[1]

Lastly, *an aggressive spirit against hostile forces* characterized the kings of prayer (2 Chronicles 32:20; 2 Kings 20:1-11; Psalm 109; 1 Samuel 23:2,4; 2 Samuel 2:1; 2 Samuel 5:19, 23). In this preparatory age of today, God is making large revelations and offering His grace more abundantly than ever before in order to test the faith and develop the spiritual powers of those intercessors who will be sharers of the authority and ministry of His throne throughout the coming ages.[2] The intercessor should learn to overcome hostile forces through the authority given him by Christ and thus prepare for co-reigning in the ages to come.

The kings play a vital spiritual role in the understanding of prayer in the life of an intercessor. It would be a great mistake not to visualize the office of the king as a spiritual office like that of a priest and a prophet.

Chapter 8
The Period of the Prophets

The Period of the Prophets is concerned with how to pray as intercessors with discernment into people and events. There are over sixty prophets mentioned by name in the Bible. This number does not include groups like the one hundred prophets that Obadiah hid in a cave and certainly not the four hundred-fifty false prophets on Mt. Carmel. It is interesting to note that there are more prophets mentioned by name than patriarchs, judges, kings, apostles or priests. The prophets fall into several categories: oral, writing, pre-exilic, exilic, post-exilic, major, minor, true, false, male and female.

A prophet is defined as a Spirit-anointed messenger of God bringing God's Word to man. Arthur Fawcett has defined the prophet best by saying that the prophet is a manifestation of God's activity.[1] In understanding the prophet, some guidelines should be kept in mind. First, a prophet is one who is ordained by God (Jeremiah 1:5). A prophet is not selected after a questioning period. He is not selected by men laying their hands upon his head. He is selected by God placing His hand upon his life. He is anointed, not appointed!

Secondly, a prophet is one who shares the foreknowledge of God (Amos 3:7). It has been said that whatever God expects His people to do, God expects His prophets to motivate them to do it. Thus, the prophet becomes a forthteller alongside of his being a foreteller. One of the credentials of a true prophet is that he is predictive in the nature of his messages and must be one hundred percent accurate.

Thirdly, the prophet is one who is known by God and man as a prophet (Ezekiel 33:33). God sends His prophets in order to give man the message from on High. God also sends His prophets in order to remove any excuse that man may claim for his defeated spiritual condition. God has allowed His prophets to walk among men for judgment's sake.

Lastly, the prophet is one who is primarily a man of prayer (Jeremiah 27:18). Prayer must not be prominent in his life, but pre-eminent! The prophets are to teach men to pray with discernment concerning the events around him and the lives of the individuals for whom God has burdened him to pray. In the following pages, a study of the prophets will be divided into oral, major and minor prophets.

Oral Prophets

Elijah

The oral prophet Elijah illustrates how to pray as an intercessor with discernment. He demonstrates several principles of intercession that produce this valuable asset.

Discern God's Will Through Private Time With Him

Elijah spent much time alone with God. It was during this time that he learned how to restrain natural forces in order to control the events of his day. There is no substitute for this private time with God, if the intercessor is to be effective in prayer.

Discern The Root Cause Of Events

The intercessor should discern and pray for the solution concerning events that surround him. Elijah had deep insights into the binding of Israel's financial strength. This great prophet brought about a national famine, which in turn, brought about the financial collapse of a corrupt nation. The people of Israel had to acknowledge that God was far greater than their financial securities. The intercessor should seek discernment into the solutions of local and national difficulties. He should then seek to bind and restrain the sin of these situations.

Discern The Root Sin In Individuals

The intercessor should further discern and pray for the

individuals involved in the events around him (1 Kings 18:15-46). Elijah discerned Ahab's weakness. Abah had a greater loyalty toward his wife than he did for the true God. Elijah challenged this loyalty. Individuals influence events. Thus the intercessor's prayers influence the events by praying for the individuals involved in them.

Discern The Proper Prayer Partner

Furthermore, the intercessor should discern and pray for others to join him in the work of intercession (1 Kings 19:19-21). Elijah chose Elisha to join him in the prophetic ministry. Today the intercessor should seek out others who have a commitment to prayer and enlist their participation.

Demonstrate Determination To Bring About God's Will

The intercessor should, like Elijah, be steadfast in his determination to bring an overthrow to God's enemies. Elijah demonstrated his determination by challenging the four hundred fifty false prophets of Baal to a contest on Mount Carmel. The intercessor should be just as determined to bring about victory for God.

Demonstrate Confidence Through Recognition Of Purpose

Also, the intercessor should realize his uniqueness in God's economy. Though Elijah was not alone in the ministry of intercession, he did have a unique role (1 Kings 19:8-18). Elijah was the key figure in the contest with the false prophets of Baal. Seven thousand others were supportive of Elijah's ministry and he did not even realize it! The intercessor should recognize his uniqueness. Christianity is a minority in the world today. The genuine believer stands as a minority within that minority. Within this select group is a smaller group that is disciplined to pray. Thus, even among the genuine believers, there are few that have seen the need to place prayer as the priority of their lives. Among this even smaller group, there are but a few that have seen intercession as their ministry and have learned the great principles of intercession. Elijah did just that.

The Lord richly honored Elijah for his recognition of his uniqueness. More is mentioned in the New Testament about Elijah than any other prophet of the Old Testament. Elijah was great in his prayer life. It was Elijah who restrained the rain for three and one half years. It was Elijah who caused it to rain again. It was Elijah who prayed down fire from heaven. It was Elijah who was caught up into heaven in a fiery chariot. In James 5: 17-18, the writer gave this epitaph concerning Elijah: "he prayed" and "he prayed again."

Major Prophets

Isaiah

Isaiah, a Major Prophet, illustrates how to pray as an intercessor with discernment into people and events. Isaiah was the prophet to the kings. He mixed well with the rulers of his day and was often called upon when there was a national crisis (Isaiah 32:20). A study of Isaiah will reveal five instances of how Isaiah illustrated the ministry of intercession. These opportunities will reveal rich insights and principles for the intercessor of today.

Pray For Those Who Are Close To The Problem

In 2 Chronicles chapter thirty-two, Isaiah prayed for Hezekiah's victory over Sennacherib, the King of Assyria, and over Hezekiah's sickness. Thus, the intercessor should pray for those who are directly affected by problems. The thrust and concentration of the prayer should not be concerning those who stand on the periphery but for those in the middle of the conflict. The intercessor should also pray for discernment in seeing both the cause of and the solution to the problem.

Pray With Those Who Are Close To The Problem

In 2 Chronicles chapter thirty-two, Isaiah not only prayed *for* Hezekiah, he prayed *with* Hezekiah as he contested against the king of Assyria. Although the intercessor may not be directly affected by the problem he should, however, seek out those who are involved with the problem and pray for God's solution. Those who are involved with the problem may be able to share helpful information that will aid in formulating the intercessor's prayer. On the other hand, as the intercessor prays with those involved with the problem, he has the opportunity to reveal to them the root cause and God's solution through the spiritual dynamic of prayer.

Pray With An Understanding Of God's Written Word

Isaiah chapter thirty-seven demonstrates how Isaiah prayed with Hezekiah and then discerned both the cause (verses 22-34) and the solution (verses 35-38) to his problem from the words of the Lord (verses 21-22). Today, the intercessor should follow the same example. The main sources of discernment are prayer with those who are involved with the problem and a basic understanding of Scriptural principles.

Pray With The Confidence Of Knowing God's Will

The intercessor should further pray from the uniqueness of being an intercessor. In Isaiah 45:11, God tells Isaiah to ask Him of things to come concerning his will. Then He tells Isaiah to command Him to do those things! The intercessor is in the unique position before God! The Lord has invited the intercessor to command Him concerning implementing His will! What an overwhelming position for a mere human being!

Pray For Renewal

Much of the focus of Isaiah's ministry was the promise of renewal. In Isaiah 45:14-25, Isaiah prophecies that renewal will come. This renewal will come through the Suffering Servant (Isaiah 53) and the Spirit of the Lord (Isaiah 61:1) in response to the intercessor's prayers (Isaiah 65:24). God's plan for renewal today is the same. It is easy as an intercessor to become preoccupied with the burden of problems and sin and to neglect the hope of renewal. Isaiah shows the intercessor how to balance the two.

Jeremiah

Jeremiah was the great weeping prophet of God to the people of Judah during the days of King Josiah. This priest-prophet illustrated various principles of intercession as he prayed with discernment into the people and events of his day.

Be Sensitive To God's Heart

Jeremiah was sensitive to God's call upon his life and God's direction for his ministry. His sensitivity is demonstrated by the constant reference to his lamenting over Judah. His intimacy with the Lord allowed him to comprehend the deep emotions of God's response to the sin of Judah. Only through such intimacy with the Lord can the intercessor share such burdens.

Be Sensitive To Changing Circumstances

The first several chapters of Jeremiah reveal that Jeremiah certainly understood the people and events to which he was called to minister. He began his prayers for repentance and change, but eventually Jeremiah realized that judgment was imminent and he ceased to pray *for* Judah and began to pray *against* the nation (Jeremiah 7:16; 11:14; 14:11). Although situations around Jeremiah were constantly changing, he continued to minister and pray faithfully. It takes a great deal of spiritual maturity in prayer to surrender to God's inevitable judgment and to pray for it. Jeremiah paid the price of ridicule and isolation by praying faithfully as God gave him discernment.

Like Jeremiah, the intercessor of today should be willing to pay the price to be faithful to the discernment God gives him. He must be alert to the circumstances that are constantly changing. He must be willing to suffer through temporal judgment for eternal purposes.

Be Sensitive To God's Eternal Purposes

Jeremiah prophesied seventy years of desolation (Jeremiah 25). No wonder he is called the weeping prophet! Yet he did not neglect the hope of restoration (Jeremiah 23:1-8; 29:10-19; 30:131; 33:1-26). He was not bitter or critical concerning God's people. He merely viewed the imminent events as days of chastisement with the hope of renewal. The intercessor gains his courage to pray for judgment through his understanding of God's eternal purposes.

Daniel

Ezekiel 14:14, 20 and Ezekiel 28:3 indicate that Daniel was considered by Ezekiel to be a great intercessor in the category with Noah and Job. The intercessor will be wise to study Daniel to gain insights into how this great man of prayer prayed with discernment into people and events. His praying takes the intercessor into rarely experienced prayer principles.

Maintain A Disciplined Time And Place For Prayer

While living in a foreign land as a political prisoner, Daniel displayed an overwhelming discipline in his daily time of prayer. Daniel 6:10 describes in detail that Daniel prayed three times a day, on his knees, facing Jerusalem, and giving thanks to His God just as he had done before his capture by the Babylonians.

It is strange and sad that we organize virtually everything except our religious life! The average believer organizes his study, his meals, his recreation, his sleep, and even his personal grooming; yet he leaves the needs of his soul to be met by chance. No one who organizes three meals a day for his body can say that he cannot possible fix a daily time for Bible meditation and prayer. Such an affirmation is a loud advertisement of spiritual indifference.[2] It is common for believers to be in a religious hurry in their devotions. In his book, *How to Pray*, R. A. Torrey wrote, "A man or woman who does not spend much time in prayer, cannot properly be called a follower of Jesus Christ."[3] The intercessor's maturity should be measured out by hours. The more mature, the more time will be spent with the Lord in prayer! Daniel's disciplined prayer life reflects much maturity!

Remain Consistent In Prayer Even Under Pressure

Daniel prayed when it was not easy to pray. The sixth chapter of Daniel describes when the princes in Babylon became jealous of the favor Daniel received from their king, they decided that the only way they could harm him was to attack his disciplined prayer life. They motivated the king to sign a decree forbidding anyone to pray or make request to any god other than the king. Daniel remained consistent even with the threat of being put in a den of lions!

Daniel's example gives new definition to a disciplined prayer life! This prophet challenges the intercessor to faithfulness in the midst of any obstacle.

Employ God's Word In Praying

The prophets are consistent in showing the intercessor the great value of using God's Word in prayer, and Daniel is no exception. It is while he is praying through the words written by Jeremiah that Daniel realizes God's plan for the Jewish people (Daniel 9:2).

The intercessor should be familiar with the Bible and should use it effectively in prayer. He also should be cautious about those that advocate strong Bible studies to the neglect of prayer. This group often seems to defend and justify the lack of prayer by spending time being in the Word. The difficulty comes when these Bible students know more about the Word of God than they know about the God of the Word. There are many who are strong in Bible study and weak in prayer. There are few, though, that are strong in prayer and weak in Bible study. In order to be effective in prayer, one must be strong in his knowledge and application of the Word of God.

The intercessor should seek to develop a spirit of prayer (Daniel 6:10; 1 Thessalonians 5:17) during his time in the

Scriptures. Although he had a strong grip on the Word of God, Daniel made prayer the priority of his day. His whole day was scheduled around his prayer times. The great writer in the area of prayer, Paul Billheimer, has stated that prayer should be the main business of each day.[4] Since prayer is the on-the-job training for ruling, then one's failure to pray is frustrating God's high purpose of the ages.[5]

Identify With Sinners Through Intercession

Daniel 9 records an unusually mature prayer of intercession by Daniel for his people. In their captivity, they had neglected their relationship to God. As Daniel intercedes for them while fasting and covered with sackcloth and ashes, he identifies with their sins of iniquity, doing wickedly, and departing from God's precepts and judgments. He uses the word "we" as he makes these confessions. Here was the man of great prayer discipline identifying with the sin of prayerlessness of his people! The mature intercessor becomes more and more like his Savior as, even in his innocence, he takes on the sins of others.

Expect Satanic Hindrance To Receiving Answers To Prayer

Daniel 10 provides a most unusual prayer experience in the life of Daniel. He had asked the Lord to clarify his understanding of His plan for the Jewish people, but he had been waiting for God's response in mourning and fasting for three full weeks. Finally an angel appears to him in response to his prayers. The angel explains to Daniel that God heard his prayers at the beginning of the three weeks, but that there had been warfare in Heaven as Satan opposed his coming (Daniel 10:12,13). A serious intercessor will meet with Satanic hindrance to receiving answers to prayer, but his persistence and patience will prevail.

Expect Wisdom Beyond Comprehension

When Daniel's prayer is finally answered and an angel

comes to tell him exactly what will happen in the end times to the Jewish people, the truths are beyond Daniel's comprehension (Daniel 12:8). He is told to shut up the words and seal the book until the time of the end (Daniel 12:4). When the intercessor becomes so intimate with God, God may reveal to him such deep truths that he will not be able to understand. When the intercessor experiences such mystery, he can trust in the words given to Daniel that he may even rest in death before the fulfillment of his knowledge is comprehended (Daniel 12:13).

Minor Prophets

Habakkuk

Habakkuk perhaps should be designated as "The Prophet of Prayer." Over one third of the Book of Habakkuk is his prayers. After struggling with God's purposes, this prophet formulated one of the most beautiful prayers in the Bible. In chapter three, his prayer can be divided into three separate parts. The first part, verses one through three, is a *cry of Habakkuk for God to revive His work in the midst of his lifetime*. The second part, verses four through nine, is the prophet's *cry for God to remember His mercy and His triumphs concerning Judah*. The last section, verses ten through thirteen, is Habakkuk's *cry to God to restore the nation of Judah* to its once enjoyed splendor. The climax of the prayer is in verses seventeen and eighteen. In these verses, the prophet acknowledges that he will keep on trusting God even though God fails in answering his prayers and wishes. In these verses the prophet illustrates how to pray with discernment. In fact, this whole chapter reveals some deep principles of prayer for the intercessor.

Intercede For National Revival

Like Habakkuk, the intercessor should pray and discern the status of a nation with regard for its need for a revival. Habakkuk evaluated his nation and felt that Judah was in desperate need of reviving. The nation was on a downhill slide morally, economically, and spiritually. Habakkuk was correct in praying for a revival. The intercessor of today, should discern his own nation concerning the need for a revival.

Praise For Past Blessings

Also, the intercessor should recall the nation's past and pray that God would cause the nation to remember as He remembers. The history of God's people was full of examples of miracles and workings of God in their midst. Habakkuk recounts them in his prayer. God's intercessor should seek to know the awakenings and the workings of God in the history of his nation. Then he should bring that information before the people and before God. If God has worked within a particular nation, it may be that He would be gracious enough to remember and work with those people again.

Intercede For National Restoration

The intercessor should pray that God would restore a nation that is in trouble. The nation of Judah at the time of Habakkuk was in serious jeopardy. The enemy had intentions of devouring the nation of Judah. Habakkuk interceded concerning his nation and requested God to restore the nation as it was before.

The intercessor should seek not only a reviving of God within the boundaries of his nation, but also a restoring of that nation to its fundamental foundations. Only this will bring about any lasting results. Many nations of the world today need a restoring more than they need a reviving.

Stand Firm When God Responds With Judgment

Habakkuk's deep intercession for revival and restoration to the people of Judah did not meet with favorable response. God did not grant his prayer. It is difficult for an intercessor not to have his prayer answered as he desires. When Habakkuk's prayer was not answered and he learned of the judgment to come, he became physically ill (Habakkuk 3:16). Yet he resolved to take his focus off of all the defeats of judgment and to refocus on the Lord. He ends his book by rejoicing in the Lord (Habakkuk 3:18,19).

Jonah

Jonah also illustrates how a Minor Prophet prayed with discernment into the people and events of his day. He was the first missionary prophet and the prophet that ran from God's call to preach to the ruthless, heathen country of Assyria. After running into difficulty, Jonah prayed a very sound and Scriptural prayer. It is obvious that Jonah was quite steeped in Bible knowledge. He knew how to pray using the Word of God that had been built into his life. His prayer in chapter two, yields several principles for the intercessor today.

Examine Yourself For Personal Bitterness Or Rebellion

First, the intercessor should overcome his personal bitterness and rebellion toward God. Because Jonah understood his calling to be a prophet to Judah, he became confused and bitter against God for calling him to preach to the nation of Assyria. This rebelliousness would only lead Jonah into further difficulty. The intercessor needs to discern if there is any bitterness within himself against God that would render his ministry worthless. This bitterness will limit his discernment. Also, the intercessor should repent of this rebellion. In chapter two of Jonah, the prophet confessed that he had rebelled and needed deliverance, but he also repented of his bitterness. It is one thing to confess and it is another to repent of the thing confessed.

Employ Scripture In Prayers

The intercessor should pray prayers that are Scriptural. There is probably no more Scriptural prayer in the Word of God than this one in chapter two of Jonah. The prophet was dependent upon God's Word as is seen in his use of the Scriptures to formulate his ideas: Psalm 130:1,2; 120:1; 18:4-6; 22:24; 69:1; 88:6; 42:7; 31:22; 69:1,2; 116:3; Isaiah 38:10; Psalm

16:10; 142:3; 77:10-11; 18:6; Jeremiah 10:8; Psalm 50:14,23; Job 22:27; Psalm 3:8; Isaiah 45:17. The prophet was saturated with the Word of God to the extent that when he was in the fish's belly he could pray such a prayer. The intercessor should saturate the Word of God throughout his system: his mind, his will, his emotions, and his spirit. The intercessor should attempt to base his prayers upon the Word of God.

Expect God To Use You In His Answer

The intercessor should pray out of trust and commitment as the prophet Jonah did. The prayer of Jonah reflects a great deal of trust and commitment to God's forgiving and showing mercy. This same commitment should characterize the prayers of God's intercessor. He should be available to fulfill his own prayers if God so leads. Jonah was ready and available to fulfill his vows and announce the salvation of his God. Jonah was willing to fulfill his own prayer. The intercessor who is sensitive enough to pray over the matter may be the very person with enough sensitivity and discernment to fulfill that prayer. The intercessor should not only be available and willing to fulfill his prayers, but should also be expecting God to call upon him to do that very thing.

Chapter 9
The Period of Christ

The Biblical period of Christ is concerned with how to pray more effectively by following Christ's example as the great intercessor. In considering the Patriarchs (Job, Abraham, and Moses) one will notice the foundation of intercession being laid out so beautifully through their examples. The Judges (Samson and Samuel) pointed out the need for the Spirit's empowering in the area of prayer. The period of the Kings (David, Solomon, and Hezekiah) took an advance upon the Judges in teaching one to pray from the perspective of authority. The Prophets (Elijah, Isaiah, Jeremiah, Daniel, Habakkuk and Jonah) demonstrated greater increase in understanding as they illustrated prayer with discernment. In coming to Jesus and His prayer ministry, one will reach the climax in understanding prayer. Jesus is the most knowledgeable person to teach on prayer. His whole life was built around prayer. An adequate look at Christ's teachings on and practice of prayer would require an addition book. Here the exploration of this division of Christ in the epic of the Scriptures will focus on the Pre-existent, the Earthly, and the Ascended Christ.

The Pre-existent Christ

The example of the Pre-existent Christ illustrates how to pray more effectively. To confirm that prayer is the primary ministry of the Ascended Christ is simple enough to do. The Scriptures are plenteous to support such a claim. Likewise, to demonstrate that the praying of Jesus reflected the priority of His earthly life is easy enough. These will be looked at momentarily. To confirm the prayer ministry of the Pre-existent Christ is a bit more difficult. Hebrews 13:8 indicates that Christ is changeless throughout the course of time and eternity. Jesus in John 17:5 requested that the Father restore the glory to Him that was once His before the worlds were created by the Word of God. John indicates that this Word of God is Jesus as referred to in chapter one of his Gospel. Perhaps by inference it should be concluded that the primary ministry of Jesus before His existence in human flesh is the same as it was while He was in the flesh and indeed the same as it is now following His ascension. Since this is the case, three precepts become evident.

Make Prayer A Priority

First, like the Pre-existent Christ, the intercessor should make prayer a priority of his life. Because this was the priority of Jesus' ministry before the Incarnation, the intercessor should recognize its importance.

Be Creative Through Prayer

The intercessor through his prayers should also bring events into existence. Through Jesus' prayers, all things were brought into existence. The intercessor controls the creativity of events in the world today. John Wesley said, "God does nothing but in answer to prayer."[1] E.M. Bounds also agrees with this in stating that God shapes the world by prayer.[2]

Be Controlling Through Prayer

The intercessor should control the events in the world through his prayers. Christ held the events of the world together through His intercession. Today's intercessor should be no different than the Master.

The Earthly Christ

The example of the Earthly Christ illustrates how to pray more effectively. In Hebrews 5:7 (NAS) the writer speaks of Jesus, who "In the days of His flesh, when He offered up both prayers and supplications with loud crying and tears to Him who was able to save Him from death, and who was heard because of His piety." The Earthly Christ undoubtedly was a praying man. In Isaiah 50:4, Isaiah spoke of the Messiah as one who awakens the ears of the God of the universe with prayer each morning. For the intercessor of today, a few conclusions are evident.

Make Prayer A Priority

Over twenty-five times the Bible speaks of Jesus praying and often Jesus spoke about prayer. If Jesus needed to spend much of His earthly life in prayer before the Father, so much more should the individual believer. Prayer was the priority of Jesus' earthly life.

Control Events Through Prayer

During His life on earth, Jesus controlled the events around Him through prayer. This will become very obvious as one looks at the chronology of Jesus' prayers and the chronology of the events in which Jesus found Himself. As the intercessor is placed within situations to which he must respond, he should control the events through prayer. Prior to every major event in the life of the Earthly Christ, Jesus would be found in prayer. Indeed, it is His prayers that brought on the events. Prayer creates crisis and conflicts.

Train Others In Prayer

Like the Earthly Christ, the intercessor should train others in prayer. Jesus spent a great deal of His teaching time on prayer. He would often pray out loud in front of His disciples in order that they might learn to pray properly. Since prayer is the on-the-job training for overcoming and ruling in the Heavenlies, it comes as no surprise that Jesus would spend so much time and effort training His disciples in the area of prayer.

The Ascended Christ

The example of the Ascended Christ illustrates how to pray more effectively. Hebrews 7:25 states, "Hence also He is able to save forever those who draw near to God through Him, since He always lives to make intercession for them." (NAS) The Ascended Christ is seated at the right hand of God making intercession for the believer. (Romans 8:34; Colossians 1:3; Hebrews 1:3, 13; 8:1; 10:12; 12:2; I Peter 3:22; Luke 22:69; Mark 12:36; Acts 2:34; Psalm 110:1; Matthew 26:64). It is a well-established doctrine that places Christ at the right hand of the Father in prayer for the believer. This indeed is the glory that Christ had with the Father before the world was made. Jesus stated in John 12:12 that He was going to the Father. In verse sixteen of the same chapter, He stated that He would be in prayer before the Father. Because of this ascended ministry of Jesus, the believer has a new relation to intercession. With these verses and others in mind, some concluding principles may be determined.

Make Prayer A Priority

Through the Ascended Christ, the intercessor is once again reminded to make prayer a priority of his life. The Ascended Jesus has had the ministry of intercession for nearly two thousand years. This far out-distances His years of earthly ministry. Nothing should contend for prayer's primary place in the life of the believer.

Intercede For Other Believers

Jesus plainly stated in the above verses that He would be praying for the believers. It is His praying that brings about victory in the every day life of the believer. The intercessor has the responsibility to control and influence the events in other believers' lives that have been brought to his attention by the Father. Indeed, the Father will use the prayers of His intercessors to bring about His desired results.

Prepare For The Marriage With The Lamb

Lastly, the intercessor should through his prayers actively

prepare for the marriage of the Bride and the Lamb. Jesus stated in John 12, that He was going to the Father and in John 14, He stated that He was going to prepare a place for the believer. In Matthew 22:1-14, Jesus spoke in a parable concerning the Marriage Supper of the Lamb. John further describes this event in Revelation 19:6-10. It is for this event that Jesus has ventured ahead of us. He is preparing the feast for the overcomer (Revelation 3:20-21). The ministry of the intercessor should be one of actively preparing for the marriage with the Lamb. This preparation involves on-the-job training in prayer and in overcoming the enemies of God.

Chapter 10

The Period of The Apostles

In Scripture, the Period of the Apostles is concerned with how to pray as an intercessor with a New Testament understanding and position. With the example of Christ before the disciples, it is evident that the disciples placed prayer as a priority in their lives and prayed with the Spirit from a position of victory. In order to understand the prayer emphasis of the Apostles, one needs to look at the prayers in the Book of Acts, the prayers by the Apostle Paul in Acts and throughout his writings, and the prayers of other Apostles, especially James.

The Apostles in Acts

In eighteen out of twenty-eight chapters in the Book of Acts, Luke speaks of prayer by the Apostles. These prayers are not vocalized for the reader. In fact, there is not a single prayer worded in the twenty eight chapters of Acts.[1] This omission does not diminish the fact of the priority of prayer in the lives of the Apostles. The emphasis on prayer by the Apostles does reveal several principles on intercession.

Pray For The Filling And Power Of The Holy Spirit

The disciples remembered the teachings of Jesus concerning the role of the Holy Spirit in prayer (John 14). Jesus had told them that the Father would give the Spirit to those who asked Him. (Luke 11:1-13). In Acts 2, the disciples waited for the promise of the Holy Spirit in an attitude of prayer. It is amazing that Jesus left this planet and rested His hopes for world evangelization upon a small church prayer meeting of 120 attending members. This small group was only a portion of the more than five hundred that had witnessed the resurrection of the living Lord. These disciples, though, prayed for the promise of the Savior. After ten days they received the expected Holy Spirit into their lives and ministry. The intercessor of today needs the Spirit's anointing in the same way that the early Apostles needed Him. One cannot expect a spiritual ministry apart from Him.

Participate In Corporate Praying

Corporate prayer was a way of life for the Apostles in the Book of Acts (Acts 1:4, 24; 2:41;4:24,31; 6:6; 7:60; 8:15; 12:5, 12; 13:3; 14:23; 16:13; 20:36; 21:5; 22:17). It becomes obvious that the disciples prayed corporately and gained mutual encouragement and an increased power in their ministry. The intercessor of today should seek opportunities to pray corporately, especially with those who are knowledgeable of prayer. He should not neglect corporate prayer, even though often it is a far cry from the corporate prayer that the disciples may have experienced.

Keep Time In Prayer And Time In The Word In Proper Balance

The disciples made practical provision to guard their time for prayer and the preaching of the Word (Acts 6:4). The Bible contains this theme often, but it is one that is neglected among the modern ministries. The Apostles sought a balanced ministry by placing prayer first and the ministry of the Word as a natural outgrowth of prayer. Prayer and the Word must go together. One is not complete without the other. How often is the ministry of the Word incomplete because of the neglect of prayer! The intercessor should maintain a proper balance.

Make Prayer A Priority

Furthermore, prayer should be the priority of the intercessor as it was with the Apostles. In the Book of Acts, Luke mentions Paul (9:4-6), Peter (10:9; 9:36-43), Stephen (7:54-60), Cornelius (10:1-6, 30-31), Lydia (16:13-16), and Silas (16:16-25) as individuals that prayed. It is interesting to note the great significance of this principle of prayer. It is communicated in every division we have examined of the Sacred Scriptures. Such a repeated theme should not be overlooked!

Value The Church As A Place Of Prayer

Throughout Scripture the meeting place of God's people is viewed as a House of Prayer (Acts 3:1; 22:17; Matthew 21:13; Isaiah 56:7). The Apostles embraced the Temple as their House of Prayer and often went there at its established prayer hours. In the twenty second chapter of Acts it is evident that the Apostles sought out the Temple as a place of prayer some thirty years after the crucifixion of Jesus! Today, the Church should be a place of prayer. E.M. Bounds was correct in his evaluation of the Church: "Any church calling itself the house of God, and failing to magnify prayer; which does not put prayer in the forefront of its activities; which does not teach the great lesson of prayer; should change its teaching to conform to the Divine pattern or change the name of its building to something other than a house of prayer."[2] Again, Paul Billheimer is very dogmatic in stating, "Any church without a well-organized and systematic prayer program is simply operating a religious treadmill."[3] The genuine intercessor must value the church in this way. Oh, how this is a neglected ministry among believers today!

Paul

The life of Paul demonstrates how to pray as an intercessor with a New Testament understanding and position. Much could be said about Paul and the ministry of prayer. Paul wrote twice as many epistles as all the other Apostles added together. There are eight times as many prayers in his epistles as in all of theirs.[4] Several prayer principles are evident in Paul's life and teachings.

Celebrate A Conversion Prayer

Paul's life demonstrates how God can turn a rebellious Pharisee into a praying Apostle! The method that God used to bring about this great change was the prayer life of a startled persecutor (Acts 9:4-6). Every intercessor should be able to trace his own conversion to his first real prayer. In reality, every believer comes to Christ through a prayer-shaped door. That original prayer of the intercessor solidifies not only his conversion experience, but also his first step in learning to co-reign with his Lord.

Put Greater Emphasis On Spiritual Rather Than Temporal Prayer Requests

An examination of Paul's recorded prayers clearly shows he very seldom prays for temporal or material things.[5] Examples of this principle are easy enough to find: Ephesians 1:15-19; 6:18-20; Colossians 4:3 are just a few of his prayers that confirm this principle. The intercessor should constantly be evaluating his prayers to see where his concentration is being placed: spiritual vrs material; eternal vrs temporal; and global vrs local. Too often the person of prayer becomes overloaded with prayers for physical, material, and temporal things. While these are not forbidden prayer requests, they can become so burdensome to force neglect of the spiritual, eternal, and global needs. As Paul's prayers demonstrate, many times the physical, material, and temporal needs can be motivations for praying spiritual and eternal requests.

Pray Specifically

Paul's prayers are never general ramblings. They are specific. Much of praying today is worded in vague terminology like "Lord, bless the missionaries." The intercessor who expects specific answers to his praying should learn to pray specifically.

Give Priority To Interceding For Others

Paul prays for others far more than himself as seen in all but one of his prayers (2 Corinthians 12:7-10). A quick glance at Paul's prayers will reveal a concern for people. He was at heart an intercessor. Today's intercessor should soon turn from prayers concerning himself and spend his time in prayer for others. It is to this end that God has raised up the intercessor.

Other Apostles (James)

Prayer is evident in the lives of the other Apostles: Jude (Jude 20, 24, 25), John (1 John 1:9; 5:14-15; Revelation 1:10; 8:4; 19:108), and Peter (1 Peter 3:7, 12; 4:7; Acts 10:9; 3:1). James, perhaps more than the others, demonstrates how to pray as an intercessor with a New Testament understanding and position.

Ask God For Wisdom

James encourages believers to pray for wisdom (James 1:5-7). The content of his book indicates that he indeed received the answer to this prayer for himself. The intercessor should become humble and request wisdom and discernment. Only in this regard can he pray intelligently and effectively.

Guard Against Prayerlessness

It is so easy to let the discipline of prayer slip away. The press of time demands and even the distraction of good things can quickly destroy the discipline. This loss does not come without a great price! James indicates that prayerlessness was the cause of divisions within the body of Christ (James 4:1-2). Prayerlessness should never characterize the intercessor.

Intercede For The Sick

James teaches that the key to physical good health is prayer (James 5:13-18). If one should become ill, he should seek out praying elders within the Church to come and pray with him. The prayer of faith will bring healing to the one who is ill. The intercessor should understand the ministry of prayer and how it relates to physical well-being. One might recall that the first mention of prayer in the Bible was in the context of Abraham praying for the health of Abimelech (Genesis 20:7). This should encourage the intercessor to pray for healing.

Pray With Faith

The example of Elijah is used by James to address the question of what kind of prayer is effective. It is trusting and committing prayer that is truly effective. The intercessor should pray with faith. Doubting prayer is defeating. It does not ascend to the Father. Only the prayer of faith can work effectively (James 5:15-18).

Live A Righteous Life

James goes on to indicate the only type of man who can pray in faith is the man who lives a righteous life (James 5:16). Confession of sin and a commitment to righteousness are of great importance in the life of the intercessor. Neglect in this area will only bring defeat in accomplishing the blessed task of learning to co-reign with the Lord.

Conclusion

While this book has sought to give an overview of the Biblical epic of prayer, so much more about prayer is found in Scripture. The next book in this series, entitled *Recapturing the Biblical Example of Prayer*, will explore extensively Jesus' teachings on and practice of prayer. The intercessor will learn some startling and often overlooked facts that will strengthen his prayer life.

Perhaps the best way to conclude this brief overview of the Biblical epic of prayer is to quote from the Berkley Version the challenging words of the Apostle Peter in 1 Peter 4:6: *The end of all things is near; therefore, be self-controlled so that you can pray!*

Endnotes

Chapter 1
[1] Paul E. Billheimer, *Destined For The Throne* (Fort Washington: Christian Literature Crusade, 1975), p. 96.
[2] Ibid., p. 15.
[3] Ibid., p. 89.
[4] Revelation 12:7-11.
[5] Isaiah 14:12; Ezekiel 28:11-19; Revelation 12:4.
[6] Romans 3:23; 5:10.
[7] Romans 8:28.
[8] Luke 10:19.
[9] Billheimer, *Destined*, p. 15.
[10] Ibid., p. 49.
[11] Ibid., p. 50.
[12] Ibid., p. 46.
[13] Ibid., p. 45.
[14] Ibid., p. 100.
[15] Erwin E. Prange, *A Time For Intercession* (Minneapolis: Bethany Fellowship Inc., 1971), p. 13.
[16] R. Arthur Matthews, *Born For Battle* (Robesonia: Overseas Missionary Fellowship, 1978), p. 18.

Chapter 2
[1] Oswald Sanders, *Satan Is No Myth* (Chicago: Moody Press, 1975), p. 7.
[2] Arthur Wallis, *Into Battle* (Fort Washington: Christian Literature Crusade, 1973), p. 8.
[3] R J. Huegel, *Successful Praying* (Minneapolis: Bethany Fellowship, 1967), p. 62.
[4] S. D. Gordon, *Quiet Talks On Prayer* (Grand Rapids: Baker Book House, 1980), p. 28.
[5] Mathews, *Battle*, p. 66.
[6] Gordon, *Talks*, p. 37.
[7] Mathews, *Battle*, p. v.
[8] Wallis, *Battle*, p. 74.

[9] Mathews, *Battle*, p. v.
[10] Prange, *Intercession*, p. 63.
[11] Danny Daniels, "The Building Up And Tearing Down Of Strongholds," *Fulness,* ll, 5 (September-October, 1979), p. 8.
[12] Corrie Ten Boom, *Marching Orders For The End Battle* (Fort Washington: Christian Literature Crusade, 1969), p. 11.
[13] Manley Beasley, "Spiritual Warfare: God's Means For Preparing Strong Christians," *Fulness,* II, 5 (September-October, 1979), p. 17.
[14] Virginia Stem Owens, *The Total Image* (Grand Rapids: Wm. B. Eerdmans Publ. Co., 1980), p. 55.
[15] Ibid., p. 47.
[16] Samuel Chadwick, *God Listens* (Westchester: Good News Publ., 1973), p. 17.
[17] Owens, *Image*, p. 63.
[18] Billheimer, *Destined*, p. 18.
[19] Beasley, *Warfare*, p. 29.
[20] Watchman Nee, *Let Us Pray* (New York: Christian Fellowship Publishers, 1977), pp. 45-46.

Chapter 3
[1] Mathews, *Battle*, pp. 90-91.
[2] Gordon Watt, *Effectual Fervant Prayer* (Greenville: Great Commission, 1981), p. 82.
[3] Mathews, *Battle*, p. 5.
[4] Ibid., p. 29.
[5] Gordon, *Talks*, pp. 111-112.
[6] Watt, *Prayer*, p. 90.
[7] Mathews, *Battle*, p. 63.

Chapter 5
[1] G. Campbell Morgan, *The Answers of Jesus To Job* (London: Lowe and Brydone, 1967), p. 17.
[2] Mathews, *Battle*, p.86.

Chapter 7
[1] William E. Barnes, *The Book of Chronicles* (Cambridge: University Press, 1899), p. xxiii.
[2] J. A. MacMillan, *The Authority of the Intercessor* (Harrisburg: Christian Publ., 1942), p. 5.

Chapter 8
[1] Leonard Ravenhill, *America Is Too Young To Die* (Minneapolis: Bethany Fellowship, 1979), p. 64.
[2] Frank Houghton and others, *Quiet Time* (Downers Grove: InterVarsity Press, 1976), p. 7.
[3] R. A. Torrey, *How To Pray* (Old Tappan: Fleming H. Revell, 1972), p. 10
[4] Billheimer, *Destined*, p. 51.
[5] Ibid., p. 53.

Chapter 9
[1] Billheimer, *Destined*, p. 17.
[2] Ibid, p. 51.

Chapter 10
[1] Arthur W. Pink, *Gleanings From Paul* (Chicago: Moody Press, 1979), p. 9.
[2] E.M. Bounds, *Necessity Of Prayer* (New York: Fleming H. Revell, 1929), p. 141.
[3] Billheimer, *Destined*, p. 18.
[4] Pink, *Gleanings*, p. 10.
[5] Wayne Mack, *How To Pray Effectively* (Phillipsburg: Presbyterian and Reformed Publ., 1978), p. 7.

Bibliography

Barnes, William E. *The Book of Chronicles.* Cambridge: University Press, 1899.

Billheimer, Paul E. *Destined For The Throne.* Fort Washington: Christian Literature Crusade, 1975.

Bounds, E.M. *Neccessity of Prayer.* New York: Fleming H. Revell, 1929.

Chadwick, Samuel. *God Listens.* Westchester: Good News Publ., 1973.

Gordon, S. D. *Quiet Talks On Prayer.* Grand Rapids: Baker Book House, 1980.

Houghton, Frank, and others. *Quiet Time.* Downers Grove: InterVarsity Press, 1976.

Huegal, E J. *Successful Praying.* Minneapolis: Bethany Fellowship, 1967.

Mack, Wayne. *How To Pray Effectively.* Phillipsburg: Presbyterian And Reform Publ., 1978.

MacMillan, Rev. J. A. *The Authority Of The Intercessor.* Harrisburg: Christian Publ., 1942.

Mathews, R. Arthur. *Born For Battle.* Robesonia: Overseas Missionary Fellowship, 1978.

Morgan, G. Campbell. *The Answers of Jesus To Job.* London: Lowe and Brydone, 1967.

Nee, Watchman. *Let Us Pray.* New York: Christian Fellowship Publishers, 1977.

Owens, Virginia Stem. *The Total Image.* Grand Rapids: Wm. B. Eerdmans Publ. Co., 1980.

Pink, Arthur. *Gleanings From Paul.* Chicago: Moody Press, 1967.

Prange, Erwin E. *A Time For Intercession.* Minneapolis: Bethany Fellowship, Inc., 1971.

Ravenhill, Leonard. *America Is Too Young To Die.* Minneapolis: Bethany Fellowship, 1979.

Sanders, J. Oswald. *Satan Is No Myth.* Chicago: Moody Press, 1975.

Ten Boom, Corrie. *Marching Orders For The End Battle.* Fort Washington: Christian Literature Crusade, 1969.

Torrey, R. A. *How To Pray.* Old Tappan: Fleming H. Revell, 1972.

Wallis, Arthur. *Into Battle.* Fort Washington: Christian Literature Crusade, 1973.

Watt, Gordon. *Effectual Fervant Prayer.* Greenville: Great Commission, 1981.

PRAYER RESOURCES

The end of all things is near, therefore be self-controlled so you can pray. 1 Pet 4:7 (Berk.)

A Christian ministry designed to serve as a resource to the Body of Christ in the arena of prayer and spiritual awakening.

We recognize that God's two-fold heartbeat for the revival of His people and the evangelization of the world is absolutely dependent upon His people being self-controlled for the purpose of prayer. Therefore, our goal is to motivate and equip believers and local congregations to pray.

We seek to accomplish this goal through a variety of ministry opportunities:
* Conducting revivals and seminars in local churches of various sizes and denominations
* Training individuals and small groups to pray
* Writing and developing materials that will aid both individual and corporate praying
* Producing and distributing tapes and books
* Consulting with a limited number of churches to establish and maintain a prayer and spiritual awakening emphasis
* Challenging the prayer lives of pastors and missionaries through conference speaking

While Dr Finley is available to conduct Missions Conferences, Pastors' Conferences, Association/Denomination-Wide Meetings, and Para-Church Group Training and Judy Finley is available to speak at Women's Luncheons and Conferences, their most fruitful ministry is conducted in local churches. Dr Finley has developed over 500 hours of prayer training and revival messages that can be used in a local church. The most beneficial meetings in a local church are those scheduled with a Sunday morning through Wednesday evening format, but there is flexibility to present some of the series in an all-day or weekend format.

www.PrayerResources.org

www.ingramcontent.com/pod-product-compliance
Lightning Source LLC
Chambersburg PA
CBHW050507120526
44588CB00044B/1724